A Histo

By Peter Francis

Cover Image © T shooter - Fotolia.com

Table of Contents

Introduction

Unlike nearly any other weapon, guns have left an undeniable mark on military and human history. Their use in warfare helped give one side a sizable advantage over the other, and their use in hunting helped early American settlers put food on their tables in a harsh new environment. But who invented them, and what were the circumstances that changed it from a cumbersome device into an essential element in warfare? Read on and discover the history of these fifteen important weapons.

Musket

From the 15th through the 17th century, large and heavy handcannons started to be replaced by the more nimble harquebus. The harquebus' curved butt stock shape gave the weapon its name from the Dutch word "hakebusse," meaning "hook gun." Like the earlier handcannons, a harquebus relied on its matchlock for firing. This early musket had several advantages over the archer's bow and quiver of arrows. Even though they weren't as accurate as a skilled archer, the harquebus was faster to fire and easier to master than the bow. Archers spent several years learning to use the longbow, but infantrymen could become proficient with the harquebus in a matter of weeks. In addition to the weapon being easier to use, harquebus ammunition—lead balls and black powder—was easier to mass-produce and more compact to carry. Toward the 16th century, bore sizes began to be standardized, making it much easier to outfit infantry because soldiers would use the same powder charge and ball size.

In the age of castle warfare, the harquebus had the added advantage of being able to be shot through small loopholes in defensive structures and the fast-moving lead projectiles weren't affected nearly as much by wind as were arrows. An intangible benefit of the early musket was its psychological effect on enemy soldiers and horses. If the enemy army fled the battlefield out of fear, that was just as effective as killing them.

Infantry in the 1500s was frequently composed of a mix of pikemen and soldiers carrying harquebus. This formation allowed the infantry to shoot and then rely on the pikemen for protection while they reloaded. The harquebus fired a projectile at low velocity and was often used against enemies protected by steel-plate armor. Good quality armor would sometimes stop harquebus ball projectiles at long range. At close range it was possible to penetrate the heaviest armor. The first response was to use thicker armor, but armor was eventually done away with altogether as muskets became more popular.

Military leaders were learning the most efficient ways to use the harqubus. Dutch, Chinese, and Portuguese armies started to use volley fire in linear formations. The front row of soldiers would fire and reload. Then the back row would step forward, fire, and reload. Using this rotating volley system, a group of infantry could sustain a steady rate of fire and protect the ranks that were reloading.

Another benefit linear formations gave was increased downrange effectiveness by compensating for the slow loading and inaccuracy of the weapons. Because of their smooth bores and generally ill-fitting projectiles, early muskets were inaccurate. A shot fired by these primitive weapons rarely hit its intended target at ranges farther than 75 yards, but if a soldier took aim at one enemy soldier and the projectile veered off its target and hit a soldier three feet to the left, the effect was still the same.

Until the mid-1500s, harquebuses were fired with a matchlock mechanism. The trigger was a long lever that, when squeezed up toward the stock, lowered the arm containing a smoldering wick onto the pan where it would ignite the priming powder. This powder flashed, sending intense heat through a tiny hole in the side of the barrel, igniting the main charge.

From the Matchlock to Flintlock

Because the matchlock was a simple design and easy to produce, it stayed in active use until the early 1700s when it was replaced by the flintlock, the most famous of which may be England's standard-issue Brown Bess musket. It was slender and lightweight and could fit a bayonet, obsoleting both the harquebus and the need for pikemen. The Brown Bess was used on both sides of the American Revolution and England used the weapon to expand its kingdom throughout the world.

A British soldier reportedly could fire three or four shots per minute with his Brown Bess, most of which had a .71-caliber bore. A soldier would bite off the end of a paper cartridge and pour some powder into the lock pan, then cast the musket about and pour the remaining powder down the barrel, ramming the undersized lead ball down on top. All that had to be done was set the lock to full cock and pull the trigger. The sharp flint in the cock slammed against the hardened steel frizzen, casting sparks down onto the priming powder.

The flintlock was generally reliable except in damp weather when moisture would render the priming powder useless. There is one account of a battle, the Battle of the Clouds in 1777 in Malvern, Pennsylvania, where American and British forces met in a field only to be greeted by a huge rain shower. With their powder ruined and not wanting to fight with only bayonets, both armies retreated.

Contrary to the popular myth, American infantrymen fought using European tactics — wearing bright uniforms and shooting from straight lines. Revolutionary soldiers didn't hide behind rocks and trees except for a few battles late in the war. In those battles, at Cowpens and Monmouth, American riflemen were able to kill British soldiers with deadly accurate fire from as far as 300 yards away.

At the time, rifled barrels were expensive to make, rifles were slower than muskets to load, and bayonets wouldn't fit on a Pennsylvania rifle — a major disadvantage in 18th-century warfare. British Major Patrick Ferguson tried to solve two of these downfalls with his rifled musket, known as the Ferguson rifle. The musket loaded from the breech, making it history's first successful breechloading firearm. The soldier would lower the gun's breech by turning the trigger guard. Then he would drop a musket ball into the barrel's back end and pour powder behind the ball. Upon closing up the breech, the musket was ready to fire.

Ferguson's rifle could be fired six or seven times per minute, could carry a bayonet, and could match the accuracy of the Americans' Pennsylvania longrifles. It could have changed the course of the war, but the rifle was too expensive to manufacture in large quantities, was fragile in the field and it never gained popularity. Major Ferguson was killed in 1780 at the Battle of Kings Mountain, shot with seven musket balls.

American forces used the Brown Bess early in the war, but began making their own weapons as the war proceeded. The Colonial government bought many Charleville muskets from France and American-built muskets up through the 1840 Springfield appear very similar to this French musket.

These smoothbore muskets continue to be generally inaccurate, reliably hitting man-sized targets at no farther than 75 yards. They could be fitted with bayonets and most battles ended after the armies had expended their 20- or 30-round cartridge boxes, with vicious hand-to-hand fighting.

Technology Advances Prove Deadly

The flintlock was widely used until the early 1800s when armies switched to the new percussion lock, which was more reliable, especially in wet weather. America's Springfield Armory produced its last flintlock muskets in 1840 and thereafter started making percussion muskets. Two years later, the armory built its last smoothbore musket.

Claude-Étienne Minié's invention in the mid-1800s of a conical shaped bullet with a hollow base changed everything about warfare. Until then, muskets had fired lead balls much smaller than the barrel's bore. This sped loading, especially as burnt gunpowder fouling built up inside the barrel, but led to the smoothbore's inaccuracy. Similarly, the Minié ball had a slightly smaller diameter than the barrel, but there were three big differences. First, the Minié ball had greased grooves that helped the soldier ram it down the barrel. Second, the projectile's hollow base allowed it to expand and grip the barrel's rifling when the gunpowder ignited behind the bullet. Third, the bullet's shape gave it a better ballistic coefficient, making it more accurate and less susceptible to crosswinds.

These advantages combined with the fact that musket builders began to put rifled barrels on their weapons to make them more accurate. With a Minié ball, a soldier with his rifled musket could reliably hit man-sized targets at 350 yards.

Technology had changed, but tactics remained the same. During the American Civil War generals still used the linear formations that had come about with the old inaccurate matchlocks. As a result, the war saw record numbers of casualties—an estimated 620,000 men were killed in battle. In comparison, 522,000 Americans were killed in both World Wars.

The percussion rifled musket was the newest best technology for only a few years. The metallic cartridge led to the replacement of the muzzleloading musket and American muskets were retooled to take cartridges. While percussion muskets were generally usable in wet conditions, muskets that fired metallic cartridges were impervious to weather as the cartridge sealed both the primer and the main charge against the elements.

When Native Americans crushed General George Custer's cavalry troops on the plains of Montana, both forces carried metallic cartridge rifles, but the cavalrymen, with their singleshot carbines were at a disadvantage. They could fire only about 10 shots per minute while Indians attacking them carried lever action Henry rifles and could fire 28 shots in the same time. Musket technology had come a long way from the primitive harquebus and changes that were still to come in the next 30 years would continue to make the battlefield an even deadlier place.

Rifle

Since 10,000 B.C. men had fought and hunted for food using bows firing metal- and flint-tipped arrows. Over time, archers learned that they could attach fletching in a twisting pattern to arrows to make them spiral and fly true in the same way that an American football quarterback throws the ball in a tight spiral to hit his receiver. It wasn't until the mid-1500s that man applied the same principle to firearm projectiles. German gunsmiths are thought to have been the first to cut rifling in gun barrels. Most of these hunting rifles were ornate works of art with relief and incise carving and metal engraving. They were short and heavy rifles known as "jaegers" after the German word for "hunt," and were bored to large calibers. The proportions allowed the rifle to balance easily. Also making these rifles balance perfectly was gunsmiths' tendency to "swamp" the barrels. Instead of forging barrels with straight sides, they would start wide and heavy at the breech, taper to narrow toward the muzzle, then flare out at the muzzle. Finer rifles had double set triggers. Pulling the rear trigger set the front as a light hair trigger, allowing the shooter to make a more careful shot.

An American Tool

When German immigrants traveled across the Atlantic to the New World, many settled throughout Pennsylvania and many brought their fatherland's rifle design with them. Gunsmiths began to pop up in Pennsylvania. Their rifles carried much of the same shaping and hardware designs that earlier German rifles did, but these Pennsylvania rifles were longer, had slender barrels, and were usually bored for smaller calibers. Historians suppose that colonists wanted rifles in smaller calibers because lead and gunpowder were expensive, sometimes an ocean away, and a smaller rifle would burn less powder.

Contemporary students of the Pennsylvania longrifle can often identify the builder of a rifle without looking on the top of the barrel where makers signed their names. Rifles' architecture — the shape of their stock, pattern of carving, width and curve of buttplate, all are particular to where they were made. Each county in Pennsylvania had differently shaped rifles as gunsmiths in each area developed his own style and taught that style to his apprentices.

Before the age of computer-controlled machines, gunsmiths used wooden rifle machines to cut rifling into the barrel. The machine's main parts were a large round wooden pole with spiral channels cut into it. These acted as a guide that twisted a steel rod when it was pulled through the barrel. Attached to the rod were small cutters that cut into the barrel's bore. After each pass, the barrel maker would add a piece of paper underneath the cutters to make them cut slightly deeper into the bore. This was a long tedious process.

Between the rifling process, the ornate carving, the engraved metal or sliding wooden patchbox, and the sights dovetailed into the barrel, rifles were expensive, usually costing about $15, a year's salary for a general laborer. Smoothbore fowlers remained popular because they were less expensive and were more versatile, handling shot for turkey and waterfowl, and buckshot and roundball for deer.

Loading the rifle was slow and careful as consistency is the key to accuracy. The rifleman would pour powder from his powder horn into a powder measure, then dump it down the barrel. He would follow this with a greased cloth patch and a soft lead ball that he rammed down. The tight patch-ball combination was important to let the rifling impart spin on the ball. The patch also acted as a seal so no gas escaped in the rifling grooves around the ball. The shooter then cocked the lock, poured fine priming powder into the lock pan and set the lock to full cock. When fired, the sharp flint in the hammer's jaws would strike against the hardened steel frizzen, showering the priming powder with sparks. The powder would flash, sending intense heat through a tiny hole in the side of the barrel, igniting the main charge.

American colonists used fewer rifles in their fight for independence than folklore would have us believe. George Washington didn't favor rifles as they were slow to load, and they didn't fit a bayonet, a crucial weakness on the 18th century battlefield. Instead of rifles, most American infantrymen carried French-made smoothbore muskets and other muskets similar to those carried by the British, and they fought in lines in open fields. Riflemen did play an important role in some Revolutionary War battles, but overall, the Pennsylvania rifle wasn't a major factor.

As flintlocks were phased out in favor of more reliable percussion caplocks in the early 1800s, gunsmiths such as John and Caleb Vincent of Ohio and Jacob and Samuel Hawken of Missouri gained notoriety as builders of shorter halfstock rifles. The Vincents made rifles in smaller calibers, while the Hawken brothers built large-bore rifles for use in the Rocky Mountains by mountain men and trappers, including Kit Carson.

The next technological advance came just in time to make the Civil War an exceedingly deadly test of America's Constitution. Claude-Étienne Minié invented a lead bullet known as the Minié ball. The bullet's conical shape gave it an increased ballistic coefficient, making it more accurate and giving it more velocity than a round ball. This new projectile combined with the fact that both sides used rifled muskets meant that linear tactics were outdated. Now soldiers could make accurate shots from as far as 350 yards.

The Changing Cartridge

In the 1830s, another Frenchman, Casimir Lefaucheux, designed and patented the pinfire cartridge, which held the powder charge and bullet. No longer did soldiers need to load powder, bullet, and cap as separate pieces. Now they were in one sealed package protected from moisture. A metal pin stuck out the side of the back of the cartridge and when the hammer hit the pin, the pin slammed into the primer, which ignited the main charge. This system remained popular for about 40 years until it was overtaken by the centerfire cartridge, which is the modern cartridge used today.

About 10 years later, the first rimfire cartridge, the .22 BB appeared. This tiny cartridge was essentially an 18-grain projectile and it evolved into the .22 Short, which launched a slightly larger projectile with black powder. Eventually the .22 Long and .22 Long Rifle cartridges were developed, the last becoming the world's most popular cartridge. The Henry rifle, used in the Civil War was chambered in .44 rimfire.

In 1866 the centerfire cartridge was born. A rifle's firing pin struck the primer, which was in the center of the cartridge's base. The primer ignited the main powder charge and the gun fired. This cartridge quickly became popular as it was adopted by pistol and riflemakers. Carbines made by Christian Sharps and Christopher Spencer were chambered in large .50-70 and .56-56 cartridges. The first number indicated the bore diameter while the second number indicated the number of grains of black powder contained in the cartridge.

The centerfire cartridge can handle powerful loads, and riflemakers built stronger rifle actions correspondingly. The bolt action became more popular and it, along with the semiautomatic actions remain the most popular for rifles today.

The Mauser bolt action, designed by Paul Mauser and first used on the Gewehr 98 in 1898 is the most popular bolt action design. The action is strong with three safety lugs, uses a three-position safety, and allows for magazine feeding. America's Springfield Armory copied the Mauser action to make its .30-06 rifle in 1903, which the country used through World War II.

Semiautomatic and Beyond

To increase soldiers' rate of fire, America began looking for an automatic rifle that would fire one shot per pull of the trigger. Canadian John Garand answered the call in 1936 with an iconic eight-shot rifle—the M1, or simply, "the Garand." General George Patton called the rifle, "the greatest battle implement ever devised." It allowed the common foot soldier to carry more firepower than his German and Japanese enemies carried in the Second World War. The rifle served the American military through Korea and until it was replaced by the M14. But the real development came in the late 1950s when Eugene Stoner invented the AR15, which would become the M16.

The M16 didn't look anything like the rifles that had preceded it. The new rifle had selective fire, meaning a soldier could fire it fully automatic or semi-automatic. Plastic instead of wood made up the rifle's stock, which made it lightweight and the rifle fitted a 30-round magazine.

Today, there are several contemporary builders of Pennsylvania rifles. Some create exacting copies of originals. They do this from either several detailed pictures, or because they're able to lay hands on the original rifle and measure every dimension. This results sometimes in the contemporary rifle being made better than the original — some originals had file marks left on the metal. Around America, shooters still compete in muzzleloader shoots. Prizes at small gun clubs are often cuts of meat, harkening back to the 1700s when a colonist might need an accurate shot to save his family from starvation.

Shotgun

Since man first began using firearms to feed and defend their families, they have experimented with shooting multiple projectiles with each shot. When fired, these projectiles spread out upon leaving the barrel and provide a pattern of impact. This spreading effect makes shotguns the gun of choice for shooters aiming at moving targets, such as birds, rabbits, and clay pigeons. The shotgun is also a popular choice of law-abiding citizens who want to protect their homes against intruders as shotguns are particularly effective at close range.

Over time, shooters began to use different size shot, or small lead balls. The way to control how fast this shot spreads out once it leaves the muzzle is by using a choke. A shotgun choke is a constriction inside the barrel that forces the pieces of shot into a pattern. Full choke, which provides the most constriction, produces an optimal 42-inch pattern at 40 to 45 yards. At the other end of the choke spectrum is Improved Cylinder, which gives the same 42-inch pattern at 25 yards. This is considered a more open choke and is better suited for short-range targets because the shot spreads out and forms a wide pattern quickly.

While rifles are measured by the size of their bore in fractions of an inch — called caliber — shotgun bores are measured in terms of gauge. The number of gauge means that that number of lead balls the diameter of the bore weigh a pound. The popular 12-gauge has a bore of .73 inches, but 12 lead balls of that diameter combine to weigh one pound. The same is true of 20-gauge, and 28-gauge guns. To complicate matters, the shotgun with the smallest bore, the .410, is actually a 67-gauge, but it's referred to by its bore size in inches.

Development of the Shell

Before the invention of the modern shotgun shell, the loose pieces of shot in the barrel posed a problem. If a loaded shotgun were tipped muzzle-down, the shot would fall out. There was also the issue of distributing the force evenly from the expanding gases produced by the burning powder to all the pieces of shot. A thick fiber disc was the answer to both problems. When loading, a shooter would place one of these "wads" on top of the gunpowder, and another wad on top of the loaded shot.

Early shotgun shells were made of brass and resembled rifle cartridges. At the shell's top was a cardboard overcard, which, like the wad in a muzzleloading shotgun, held the powder and shot in place. In the late 1870s paper shells started replacing brass and the top of the shell was tightly folded into the center, eliminating the need for the overwad. All-brass shells were common for the next hundred years until the plastic became the material of choice for ammunition makers. The shell's base is brass and contains a centerfire primer and rim so a gun's extractor can yank the spent shell from the chamber. Above the main powder charge is a plastic compression wad. When the gun fires, the wad travels down the barrel with the shot, sealing in the gases to give the shot as much velocity as possible.

With the cost of rifles equaling a general laborer's yearly salary, smoothbore fowlers and trade guns were popular in American colonies. In addition to their attractive price, smoothbores were versatile. They could be loaded with small shot for birds, larger pellets for rabbits and pheasants, and buckshot for deer at close range. Fowlers also shot roundballs accurately to about 75 yards. It was a waterfowl hunter, Alexander Forsyth, who in 1807 patented the percussion lock. He had become frustrated that birds saw the flash of his flintlock and flew off before the gun ignited.

Shotguns are typically used at short range, but with a solid lead slug, a modern shotgun can hit the vitals of a whitetail deer past 100 yards. In 1898 German Wilhelm Brenneke designed a lead slug to which the wad stayed attached after firing to act as a stabilizer. American Karl Foster invented the Foster or rifled slug. A typical 12-gauge Foster slug weighs 1 ounce. The slug has a hollow base and grooved sides that allow it to be shot in a choked barrel. Both the Brenneke and the Foster slug are used in smoothbore shotguns. Hunters can also use a rifled barrel for their shotgun and shoot saboted slugs. These projectiles are shaped like rifle bullets and have a plastic sleeve that grips the rifling, imparts spin on the slug, and drops off after the slug leaves the barrel. Slugs are the main tools of hunters in states where high-powered rifles aren't permitted for use on deer.

Versatility for Hunting, Fighting and Defense

This ability to shoot almost any projectile lent the shotgun to a variety of adaptations. The blunderbuss was a short-barreled, large-bore muzzleloader with a flared muzzle, making it easy to load all manner of projectiles on board a tossing ship or carriage. For close-quarters combat, there wasn't a better weapon. Loaded with rocks, nails, glass shards, and lead balls, these were sailors' and pirates' tools. When fired point blank, a shotgun loaded with birdshot will punch a hole straight through a 4"x4" wooden post. If the gun is fired from about three feet, the same ammunition cuts the post in half.

Sailors soon realized they could adapt this scattergun technique to their cannons and came up with grapeshot, a canvas bag filled with large lead balls and other projectiles. When fired, the bag ripped open and the projectiles spread out, clearing ship decks, cutting down masts, and punching holes in hulls. Armies adopted grapeshot in land warfare too. During the Civil War battle of Antietam, Union troops advanced through a field of standing corn. Confederate artillery began firing grapeshot and at the end of the day, Union Major General Joseph Hooker said the field was cut as closely as could have been done with a knife.

As Americans spread westward, the shotgun remained a popular defensive tool. Wells Fargo Company riders carried shotguns for defense against bandits and stagecoaches carrying strongboxes often had a man armed with a shotgun ride beside the driver. Since that armed guard usually carried a shortened shotgun for close-quarters defense, western movies and fiction writers popularized the phrase, "riding shotgun."

Development of Modern Actions

In the 1890s legendary firearms inventor John Browning designed the Model 1897 pump action shotgun. With this gun's success, the pump, or slide action began competing with the lever action, which had been common for rifles. The United States military adopted the Model 1897 in World War I and it proved devastatingly effective in trench warfare. The weapon quickly earned the name, "the Trench Broom," and in 1918 the Germans tried to outlaw the weapon's buckshot ammunition.

The pump action has continued to be popular with police and military forces, hunters, and target shooters. Designed in the 1950s and 1960s, respectively, the Remington 870 and the Mossberg 500, both pump shotguns, are America's most popular shotguns. Pump actions are reliable and not prone to jamming, even when snow or mud work their way into the action. Another popular shotgun action is the break-open. By pushing a button or lever, the shooter can pivot the barrel so it breaks open and exposes the breech for loading and unloading. These guns usually have one barrel or two. Over-under guns have two barrels stacked on top of each other and side-by-side guns have barrels that are beside each other. Break-open shotguns are slender and lightweight, perfectly suited for bird hunting where the hunter carries his shotgun all day. Another advantage of having two barrels is that the hunter can give himself two different chokes — one for close shots and one for farther shots. If he happens to miss a bird with the first shot and the bird flies away, the second barrel may be fitted with a tighter choke that will help him bring the bird down at a longer range.

The final shotgun action is the semiautomatic. Like with semiautomatic rifles, a shotgun with this action fires one shell for every pull of the trigger. The action uses the shell's recoil to cycle the bolt and load the next shell and in doing so does the shooter a favor by soaking up much of the shell's recoil. This is a big factor when shooting heavy duck and turkey loads or when target shooting with a case of ammunition.

Practice with shotguns usually involves shooting at clay pigeons, which are typically four-inch discs made of pitch that are launched and break apart when shot. Aside from casual practice, there are three shotgun events: sporting clays, trap, and skeet. Sporting clays involves a shooter walking to different stations where targets are presented in different patterns. One station may launch two clay pigeons rolling and bouncing along the ground to simulate running rabbits, while another station launches a clay pigeon over the shooter's head. Trap involves a single clay pigeon launcher that throws the pigeons at random angles while the shooter shoots the target from different positions. Skeet fields have two launchers, one high off the ground and one low launcher. The shooter shoots a clay pigeon thrown from each launcher as he moves to different stations in a half-moon pattern between the two launchers.

Submachine Gun

Submachine guns are small automatic rifles or carbines that fire pistol cartridges. The gun's small size makes it ideal for clearing houses and for use in close-quarters fighting, where it is maneuverable like a handgun, yet has much more firepower and is more controllable when used as a fully automatic weapon. The submachine gun is used mostly by special law enforcement units and units of the military.

The concept of creating carbines that are chambered in a pistol cartridge originated in the late 1800s when gun makers had the idea that if a man's revolver and lever rifle both fired the same round, he would need to carry only one type of cartridge. Firearms companies still build lever-action rifles in .32 H&R Magnum, .44 Magnum, and .357 Magnum, which are handgun cartridges, the latter two calibers remaining popular for self-defense, target shooting and hunting.

Heavy Machine Guns

With Hiram Maxim's invention in 1884 of a heavy 60-pound machine gun, militaries began trying to design and build a gun that possessed the firepower of a large tripod-mounted automatic weapon in a package small enough to be carried by one man. 1911 was a great year for American gun makers. Along with John Moses Browning's designing of the 1911 .45-caliber automatic pistol, fellow American Isaac Newton Lewis designed a reliable machine gun that, at 28 pounds, was a good deal lighter than the Maxim. The U.S. military didn't quickly adopt the Lewis and instead, the British armed forces pressed it into service and chambered it in .303 British instead of the all-American .30-06.

The Lewis gun used the gas from the previously fired cartridge to push the bolt rearward against a spring, allowing the next round to drop from the drum pan magazine and be pushed into the chamber on the bolt's return frontward. Besides the distinctive 50- or 100-round magazine on top of the gun, the other recognizable feature of the Lewis gun was the large cooling shroud that covered the length of the barrel. The gun was often mounted in airplanes, vehicles, and used as antiaircraft guns and is often pictured without this cooling shroud.

While the Lewis gun was a common sight on the battlefield from World War I through the Korean War, it was still heavy and big. In 1918 German Hugo Schmeisser developed the first true submachine gun, the MP 18, as an offensive weapon in the trenches. Firing the 9mm cartridge originally designed for the Luger pistol invented a few years earlier, the MP 18 used a 20- or 32-magazine and operates by blowback instead of gas. With the blowback operation, the firearm's breech doesn't lock. Instead, the fired cartridge pushes the bolt directly, using the recoil to work the action. The gun wore a simple wooden stock and a perforated metal handguard around the barrel. Its effectiveness in battle led to automatic weapons being outlawed in Germany by the Treaty of Versailles. Still, the MP 18 would influence submachine gun design for the next 40 years.

Machine Guns In Smaller Packages

America's first easily portable machine gun came in 1918, once again from the mind of John Moses Browning. The M1918 Browning Automatic Rifle, or the BAR, came at the tail end of the First World War, but in its limited service, won favor with soldiers for its ruggedness and firepower. While not technically a submachine gun, it was light enough to carry, was easy for one soldier to carry and fire, and it gave a squad enough firepower to act as an independent unit.

Weighing in at 16 pounds, the BAR was a select-fire rifle, meaning it could be shot either as a semi-automatic with one shot per pull of the trigger, or fully automatic. The wooden buttstock and forearm eventually changed to plastic during World War II as the nation's walnut trees diminished because of their use for gun stocks. Soldiers usually deployed the weapon with its bipod attached near the muzzle. It was chambered in the powerful .30-06 and could fire at a rate of 600 rounds per minute, though the double-stack magazines held only 20 rounds. The BAR used a gas from the previous shot to cycle the bolt and the weapon was striker-fired. This meant that instead of using a hammer, a striker is cocked, then released by the trigger.

Submachine Guns Are Born

The BAR was very popular with fighting men, but at the end of World War I, in 1919, John Thompson finished work on his submachine gun, the gun that became known as the Tommy Gun. Thompson had started the project with the goal of giving American soldiers a dependable tool to clear trenches. Thompson was too late for the First World War, but his gun became popular with American gangsters and outlaws like John Dillinger and Bonnie Parker and Clyde Barrow. The U.S. Marine Corps used the gun, as did the U.S. Postal Service to guard mail shipments. Like the BAR, The Thompson used a blowback operating system and fired the .45ACP cartridge—a round that's powerful when compared with other pistol rounds, but weak when compared with rifle cartridges. Firing around 600 rounds per minute, the gun fed from 30-round stick magazines that dropped below the gun and 50-round drum magazines. The gun's price held it back from major civilian sales. At the time, the gun cost about half the price of a new Ford automobile.

In addition to its high cost, the Thompson was heavy at more than 10 pounds. In comparison, the standard-issue rifle for the U.S. Infantry was the M1 Garand, which was a heavy gun in its own right, weighing nine pounds but firing the .30-06 cartridge. Another weakness was the Thompson's accuracy for targets farther than 50 yards. Because of the .45ACP's relative lack of power, it was best used in close quarters combat. U.S. Marines used it in the jungles of the Pacific, but preferred the BAR's heavier bullets that were less likely to be deflected by jungle foliage.

Cheap, Simple, Effective

As the world ramped up for the Second World War, the U.S. military was looking for a better option to replace the Thompson as a lightweight carbine for use by artillery officers, tank crewmen, and anyone who didn't use a weapon for his primary duty. George Hyde came up with an answer in 1942, designing the M3, more commonly called the Grease Gun for its resemblance to a mechanic's greaser. The M3 was cheap to make since it was made up of stamped metal with only a few welds. At eight pounds, it was lighter than the Thompson, it was more accurate than its predecessor, and fired the .45ACP.

Hyde's creation wasn't entirely original, but was a copy of the British STEN gun, designed two years earlier by Reginald Shepherd and Harold Turpin. The biggest benefit of the STEN was its low cost and England's arms makers built about 4 million for World War II. Using a blowback action, the gun had a rate of fire around 500 rounds per minute and used 32-round magazines. At just over seven pounds, the STEN was a popular newcomer to the battlefield, boosting the firepower of British soldiers who were accustomed to carrying bolt-action Enfield rifles. Like its imitator, the STEN was a very plain gun with a wire skeleton butt stock and no grip or forearm. The shooter held the stick magazine, which stuck out the gun's left side.

Unlike the STEN, the American's M3 wasn't manufactured until 1944 and only about 700,000 were made before the war ended. The Germans didn't have that problem as most of the war, they used the MP40, designed in 1938 by Heinrich Vollmer. Like the American and British submachine guns, the MP40 used a blowback operating system and a 32-round stick magazine, firing about 500 rounds per minute. At the war's beginning, the submachine gun was carried by officers and paratroopers because the gun had a wire folding buttstock. But as German leadership saw the gun's effectiveness, the gun was issued to more troops and began to replace the standard-issue Kar98 bolt-action rifle.

Development of the submachine gun slowed after the war and the next advancement didn't appear until the mid-1960s when engineers at Heckler and Koch transferred the delayed blowback operating system from the company's full-size G3 automatic rifle and created the MP5. First used in both the early assault rifle, StG45 and the heavy machine gun, the MG42, the delayed locking system was designed by Ludwig Vorgrimmler. The design works as rollers on the bolt slow its movement to the rear after a shot. The system is simple and doesn't require the barrel to recoil, which increases the MP5's accuracy because the barrel remains steady.

The gun has been so popular with military units and law enforcement that since its original design, there have been 120 different variants of the MP5. A selector switch allows the shooter to fire single shots, bursts of two or three shots, or fully automatic. Weighing just over five pounds, the MP5 fires the 9mm at up to 900 rounds per minute and uses magazines that hold up to 40 rounds.

Fully automatic firearms are not illegal in the United States, but their ownership is limited by the National Firearms Act of 1934, the Gun Control Act of 1968, and the Hughes Amendment in 1986. Would-be purchases must undergo an extensive background check and pay a $200 tax and only automatic firearms manufactured and registered with the government before 1986 can be owned or transferred.

Arquebus

Firearms development began with the invention of gunpowder in China in the ninth century. Alchemists combined charcoal, saltpeter, and sulfur into a powder they called "huo yao" and it was first used in bombs. The Silk Road trade routes moved gunpowder from China to Europe in the 13th century and gunpowder was refined and different recipes were tested before the best mixture—75 percent saltpeter, 15 percent charcoal and 10 percent sulfur—was found.

Chinese fire lances were invented in the 10th century as the first guns. These bamboo or metal tubes shot flames and various projectiles at enemies. Cannons appeared in Italy around 1320, where they were modified as European nations waged many wars. These huge artillery pieces were made with iron bars held together in a tube, similar to coopers' wooden barrels. The English forces that attacked French forces at St. Malo in 1378 used about 400 of these types of cannons.

Thanks to the invention of the matchlock ignition system in 1475, armies began translating this firepower into smaller, more portable packages, so that two men could carry one. When the shooter pressed the trigger, an arm lowered a smoldering wick into a pan of priming powder, which burned rapidly and set off the main powder charge inside the barrel. The first of these firearms in a manageable size was the arquebus.

Some historians say that the arquebus was first used by the Chinese in the mid-1300s and that by early 1500, they had spread to Europe, specifically France and Hungary. Others say that the Portuguese introduced the weapon to the Japanese, who called it a tanegashima, during the same time period. The name comes from the Japanese island where a ship with Portuguese explorers landed in 1543. The island's ruler purchased matchlocks from the Portuguese and a swordsmith began copying the ignition system and barrel. Over the next several years, Japanese gunsmiths produced some 300,000 tanegashima matchlocks.

Named For Its Shape

The arquebus, whose name is taken from a Dutch word meaning "hook gun," was a long-barreled firearm shot from the chest and the soldiers who shot them were called arquebusiers. When it was first developed, arquebus' buttstocks were straight, directing the gun's full recoil into the shooter's chest. This straight stock also made it difficult for the shooter to put his cheek directly behind the barrel to aim the weapon. German gunmakers started to cut the buttstocks so they curved downward behind the barrel's breech, effectively raising the barrel and allowing the shooter to aim. They also curved the end of the butt, making it fit the shooter's shoulder. Arquebuses with this shape were used in England and the weapon was called a hagbus, hakebut, haquebut, or bagbut, names derived from the buttstock's hooked shape.

They tended to have large bores, in the neighborhood of .70-caliber and were smoothbores. The round lead projectiles didn't fit into the bores tightly and as a result, these early firearms were extremely inaccurate. The arquebus took a minute or two to load and the delicate ignition system was very susceptible to rain and dampness. An archer could fire a quiver full of arrows in the time it took the matchlock-toting soldier to load and fire a single shot. In addition to the unreliability of the ignition system, sparks from the wick could set fire to an adjacent soldier's powder supply.

Because of these weaknesses of the new firearms, the bow remained a popular weapon. A soldier with a crossbow or longbow could fire much faster with greater accuracy and range. However, mastering the crossbow or longbow took years of practice, whereas a soldier could learn how to load, fire, and clean an arquebus in a matter of months. In its early stages of development, gunpowder was expensive, but as it grew more widely used, its mass production increased. Molding the lead ball projectiles for the arquebus was also a simple process, making the gun's ammunition easy to mass-produce. On the other hand, making arrows was still a highly skilled craft.

Because of these advantages, the arquebus grew in popularity. While members of the elite class would study for years to become a skilled swordsman or archer, a month of training could turn a lower-class soldier into a skilled gunner. And the arquebus became the trusted weapon for explorers who discovered the New World. Sailors under the command of Christopher Columbus in the late 1400s carried guns. When one of the shipwrecks associated with Columbus and his discovery of Hispaniola was discovered, matchlocks and a hand cannon were recovered from the wreckage. Spanish explorers with Juan Ponce de Leon who journeyed through the land that would become Florida probably also used these types of weapons for defense and hunting and men who companied Hernando DeSoto in his 1539 voyage to Florida carried arquebuses.

The Weapon's Weaknesses

Because ignition was slow and the gun was heavy, most were fired from a forked stick that acted as a rest. Arquebussiers carried coarse powder for the main charge and fine powder for priming the ignition system. Projectiles were usually stored in a leather bag tied at the top. And to protect himself in case the arquebussier was caught with an empty gun, he carried a sword. Between shots, the burning wick had to be removed from the matchlock and blown on or fanned to keep it lit. An assistant called a varlet sometimes accompanied arquebusiers in order to help carry all this gear and to maintain a fire to ensure the wick stayed lit.

To compensate for the arquebus' weaknesses in battle, new tactics evolved. Because of the weapon's inaccuracy, commanders would line up hundreds of men next to each other. The men would fire at the same time in the hopes that projectiles that strayed horizontally from their intended target would still hit an enemy soldier. To compensate for reloading time, tactics involved placing the arquebusiers in lines three men deep, so that after one rank shot, the row behind them could step forward and shoot. This system of rotating volleys maintained a consistent rate of fire. These concepts of volley fire and linear tactics became the norm through the mid-1800s even when technology produced deadlier weapons.

Another tactic called pike and shot was developed to help protect arquebusiers while they were reloading. In the early 1500s, as French cavalry and pikemen defeated Spanish forces, the Spanish decided to combine the arquebus' firepower with the old-fashioned but reliable pike. Instead of separating men armed with the gun from those armed with the pike, Spanish leaders formed men with both weapons into blocks so they could defend each other.

Arquebus Takes Center Stage

The arquebus' superiority was proven in battles in the first half of the 16th century as arquebus shooters protected by pikemen killed several thousand fully armored knights. As this scene replayed itself, it became clear that the arquebus was ushering in a new age of warfare, one that was less about chivalry and more about drawing a distinct line between victory and defeat. Armored knights weren't feared as they once had been when not even a well-aimed arrow could defeat a suit of armor. Now, a single projectile could kill a knight and a force of arquebus shooters could effectively repel a horseback charge.

Even in the firearm's infancy, when its usefulness was questionable, the matchlock's introduction to the Japanese battlefield brought about major changes in warfare. Japanese armies developed a system of volley fire and built protective covers to protect the ignition system, allowing the gun to fire in the rain and making it less vulnerable to dampness.

In 1567 an important leader in central Japan wrote that guns would be the most important weapons and that armies should decrease the amount of spears and arm those men with matchlocks instead. At the Battle of Anegawa in 1570 one army defeated a more powerful army by using arquebuses. Again, at the 1575 Battle of Nagashino, 3,000 gunners protected by breastworks won the day by firing volleys at enemy cavalry charges and infantry. Japanese forces also used the guns when the country invaded Korea in 1592. A quarter of the 160,000 invaders carried arquebuses. Japanese forces quickly defeated the Koreans and the invading armies captured Seoul just three weeks after landing.

While the arquebus came to rule the ancient battlefield, it would soon be displaced by a new, faster firing and lighter weapon — the musket. Muskets could fit bayonets, which obsoleted the pikeman. The new weapons were slightly more accurate and were inexpensive to produce, meaning that all infantrymen carried muskets. Tactics developed for use with the arqubus would be used, improved, and perfected in time for the American Civil War when muskets became accurate enough to hit a man-sized target from 350 yards away. Military leaders saw that new weapons didn't mix well with old tactics. No longer would armies march out in bright uniforms to meet each other on the field of battle. Instead the next war, known as the Great War, saw soldiers hunker down in series of trenches. It was a far cry from the early days of fire lances and primitive cannons.

Blunderbuss

The blunderbuss most likely originated in Holland during the latter part of the 16th century and the name comes from the English pronunciation of the Dutch word, "donderbusche," which combines the words for "thunder" and "gun."

Distinguishing Features

The blunderbuss served as an early shotgun and was typically loaded with a number of small lead balls. The gun could shoot anything that fit down the barrel, including gravel or broken glass. Dumping them all in at once, especially for military usage, was much more efficient. The gun's huge mouth also had something of a psychological effect upon the person at whom it was directed. Blunderbusses weren't equipped with sights because they were built for close-in fighting and because the huge swell at the muzzle would have blocked the view in front of the sights. The blunderbuss stands apart from other short muskets of the time because its iron or brass barrel was flared at the muzzle. This flared muzzle differentiates it from other large caliber carbines. The distinction between the blunderbuss and the musketoon is less noticeable, as musketoons were also used to fire shot, and some had flared barrels. However, musketoons remained in use and evolved into the short carbine after the blunderbuss was retired. Blunderbusses were typically short, with barrels under two feet in length, at a time when a typical musket barrel was over three feet long.

One feature of the blunderbuss that gained popularity over other guns was its flared muzzle bore. Several gunsmiths in Pennsylvania took to "crowning" the barrels of their Pennsylvania longrifles to facilitate loading. Owners of these rifles often loaded them with tight patch-ball combinations to wring out as much accuracy as possible, but this also made loading with a wooden ramrod difficult. Crowning was the process of reaming out the muzzle bore slightly to make short-starting the patch and ball easier. Then, once the ball was a few inches down the barrel, the rifle's owner could firmly ram it home.

Blunderbusses used the flintlock ignition system and their use ended in the early 1800s as the percussion ignition system became widely used. A blunderbuss used by the British mail service from 1788 to 1816 was a flintlock with a 14-inch long flared brass barrel, brass trigger guard, and an iron trigger and lock.

Close-Range Effectiveness

What the blunderbuss lacked in range and accuracy, it made up for with its blunt force on land or at sea. Ships carried the weapon for protection from pirates, who used them as well. After firing broadsides with cannons at a target ship, pirates would try to clear the deck with swivel guns and blunderbusses. Then, after these big shotguns had reduced the ship's defenses, the pirates would board.

A widespread myth says that blunderbuss's flared barrel helped the projectiles spread when they left the barrel, but this isn't the case. The main benefit from the flared muzzle was that it acted as a funnel and allowed for easier loading while riding a horse or on a swaying ship deck. Like shot fired from a shotgun, a blunderbuss's charge conformed to the main portion of the bore and remained in a condensed pattern even after leaving the barrel. The farther the shot traveled from the muzzle, the more it spread out. The one feature of the blunderbuss that helped it spread its shot charge quickly in a short distance from the muzzle was the gun's characteristically short barrel. In this way, the blunderbuss acted as a sawed-off shotgun, allowing the shot to spread to a wide pattern within 20 feet of the muzzle. Because of this excellent close-range effectiveness, the blunderbuss was perfect for home defense and it was sometimes called a stairwell gun because one blast would eliminate any number of threats coming up a flight of stairs.

The blunderbuss, also called a dragon because of the flames and sparks that would shoot out the short barrel when it was shot, was typically issued to troops such as cavalry, who needed a lightweight, easily handled firearm. The weapon became so associated with cavalry that the mounted soldiers began to be called dragoons. In 1779, George Washington wrote to the Board of War that because of their firepower, light blunderbusses were preferable to carbines for dragoons for battle. His argument said that since cavalry engages in fighting at close range, they should carry weapons specifically designed for that short-range combat.

In addition to the cavalry, the blunderbuss found use for other duties, such as for guarding prisoners or defending mail coaches, and close quarters combat. Blunderbusses were also commonly carried by officers on naval warships, privateers and by pirates for use in close-quarters boarding actions. Many blunderbusses fitted bayonets, making the weapon even more formidable as hand-to-hand fighting implements.

Small Artillery

During the American Revolution, each patrol of German rifleman, called jaegers, carried two blunderbusses. The patrols used these big-bore guns to start ambushes and to escape any ambushes they encountered. The man carrying the blunderbuss would fire his gun, and instead of waiting around to counter the ambush, the rest of the jaeger patrol would run in the direction the blunderbuss had fired. Acting as a handheld claymore mine, these guns were able to clear a substantial path because of their excessive loads. Soldiers typically loaded them with 200 grains of powder (for comparison, a typical musket was charged with about 60 grains) and 12 .50- and 22 .32-caliber balls. Together with this devastating charge, the blunderbuss sounded like a small cannon when it was fired and it created quite a bit of smoke, which helped hide the men carrying it.

A typical naval blunderbuss charge was two musket cartridges and a weakly stitched bag made of hat felt filled with shot. The heavy felt acted as an overshot wad to keep the shot in the barrel even if the barrel were tipped down. When fired, the bag would burst open, turning the blunderbuss into a shotgun. Neither this charge nor the jaegers' charges were packed down tight against the breech and the huge bore and muzzle gave a large opening for the escape, preventing the breech from exploding. But, as we know what the loads were, we don't know if the jaegers fired these loads from their shoulders. It would have packed a punch to the person shooting the gun as well as the person being shot with it.

Blunderbusses were commonly used as coach guns to discourage possible attacks from 18th and early 19th century highwaymen. A typical British mail coach would have a single postal employee on board, armed with a blunderbuss and a brace of pistols, to guard the mail from highwaymen. In 1786, a highwayman attempted to hold up a mail coach and was shot dead. No further attempts at robberies were ever reportedly made on mail coaches. Mail coach guards were the only people aboard a British mail coach allowed to carry weapons and because of that, it was difficult to be chosen for the position. Most English examples wear a coach's name stamped or engraved at the end of the muzzle or on the barrel tang on the breech end. As shotguns phased out blunderbusses, stagecoaches and express riders continued to use them for protection even as brass and paper cartridges gained popularity. Stagecoach drivers in the American West almost always carried short-barreled shotguns to ward off bandits. The Lewis and Clark Expedition carried a number of blunderbusses as light handheld artillery pieces — some of these guns were mounted as swivel guns on the crew's boats.

Limited Use In America

While the blunderbuss is often seen in artwork as a common tool of the Plymouth Colony Pilgrims in 1620, the blunderbuss was probably rarely used in the American colonies. Instead, pilgrims most likely carried matchlock muskets, some wheel locks, and early flintlocks. Someone in the New World would have very little use for a gun whose accurate range was limited to about 20 feet. He was much more likely to own a smoothbore fowling gun, which shot birdshot, buckshot, and large lead balls. After British troops under Thomas Gage occupied Boston early in the American Revolution, he ordered the residents to surrender all their firearms. Bostonians turned in only 63 blunderbusses.

Many American and European gunsmiths built blunderbusses, but the gun wasn't limited to those two continents. Gun makers in Turkey, India, and Arabia also built them and in Turkey, a short version of the gun emerged and is considered one of the earliest handguns. Even in Europe, blunderbusses weren't limited to being fired from the shoulder—some were very small handguns, while others had multiple barrels.

Light carbines took the place of the blunderbuss and as metallic cartridges became the norm and firearms were loaded from the breech, there was no longer a need for the blunderbuss's enlarged muzzle. Today we see the lasting marks that the gun left on modern firearms, mainly the short-barreled shotgun. Loaded with heavy buckshot loads, this may be the most common tool of choice for Americans wishing to protect their families.

Machine Gun

Ever since the invention of firearms, people have tried to fire more projectiles in a shorter time. The first method of doing so was with superposed loads. Mentioned as early as 1558 by an Italian writer, this method involves placing several charges of projectile and powder in a single barrel. The ignition mechanism, typically a flintlock, was moved toward the muzzle so it would fire the first load, then the shooter would move the flintlock rearward to the next charge and fire it. This method wasn't very reliable and sometimes the barrel would burst from the ignition pressures.

Early Innovations

Charles Cardiff, an Englishman, received a patent in 1682 for these types of superposed loads in a single barrel and in 1777 American Joseph Belton used the concept to patent the gun that became known as simply the Belton Flintlock. The flintlock on Belton's gun slid to set positions beside multiple touchholes. These acted as fuses so the shooter lit the first fuse, then moved the lock to the next touchhole and lit it, continuing to light the fuses to keep the gun firing. Using drawings and Belton's writings to the Continental Congress, we know that his firearm could fire as many as 20 shots in 16 seconds. While Belton tried to convince the American government, the British army, and the East India Company to purchase the firearm, it never became widely accepted.

Another early gun that fired multiple projectiles was the Puckle gun, invented in 1718 by James Puckle. The gun was essentially a tripod-mounted flintlock revolver with an 11-shot cylinder. Like the Belton Flintlock, the Puckle gun was turned down by the British military, but not before showcasing its rapid pace of fire. During public trial for the English Board of Ordnance in 1722, the gun fired 63 shots in seven minutes during a rainstorm, a feat that was unheard of at the time.

In 1779 James Wilson designed and built the Nock Volley gun. A British engineer, Wilson intended the gun to be the perfect tool for naval sailors who needed heavy firepower in a handheld platform. The Nock Volley gun used a flintlock to fire seven barrels. When fired, the lock would ignite the center barrel, which would ignite the charges in the other six barrels. Those who have fired original volley guns say the weapon deals almost as much punishment at the back end as it does at the muzzle end. Unfortunately for the British Royal Navy, this fundamental flaw was overlooked until after 500 were purchased and sailors firing them often suffered injuries. Plus, with their fearsome recoil, the guns couldn't be aimed and shot accurately. The Royal Navy realized its mistake and pulled the weapons from service after just a few years in 1804.

Around the same time, the pepperbox pistol was gaining popularity. Originally patented by Benjamin and Barton Darling of Massachusetts, the pepperbox was a single-action revolver, but instead of using a revolving cylinder to hold the main charges and projectiles, the pepperbox's barrels rotated. When the percussion hammer was cocked, the barrels would rotate. After each shot, the shooter would cock the pistol again and be ready to fire. One of the weaknesses of the pepperbox design was that the weight from the weapon's multiple barrels made it muzzle-heavy and difficult to aim. Another design flaw was that occasionally and unpredictably, one barrel firing would set off other barrels, causing a chainfire.

Samuel Colt's 1835 patent of the revolver pistol ended the pepperbox. With its revolving cylinder, the revolver didn't suffer from chainfires. It was able to be much lighter since it had only one barrel and the fact that the cylinder was removable made reloading much simpler than the muzzle-loading pepperbox. One more benefit of Colt's revolver was that it could use sights. These combined with the revolver's rifled barrel to make the new gun much more accurate.

A Miniature Army

It only took a few more years to start on the direct path toward the modern machine gun. During the Civil War, Wilson Agar developed a gun that he considered a one-man army. The Agar gun, sometimes nicknamed the Coffee Mill gun because of its appearance, was a stand-mounted gun operated by a crank. Paper cartridges, which were standard for infantry muskets, were loaded into metal tubes with a percussion cap in the rear and fed into the chamber by a hopper on top of the gun. The weapon's operator would turn the crank to feed rounds into the chamber, where a hammer would drive the firing pin into the percussion cap, firing the cartridge. The empty cartridge tube would drop from the chamber into a bin and a new cartridge would drop into the chamber. The crank also operated a blower fan that moved air through a jacket around the barrel to keep it from overheating.

The gun could fire up to 120 rounds per minute, its rate of fire limited by the speed at which the gun's crew could reload cartridges into their metal tubes. Abraham Lincoln wrote that he was impressed with the weapon, but they were rejected by the Ordnance Department for their waste of ammunition and the Agar gun didn't see much battlefield use. In addition to using ammunition too quickly, the guns didn't perform well in the field as the barrels overheated and the gun itself jammed often. Because the Agar gun fired the same bullet as the infantry's muskets, the artillery piece had the same effective range—a few hundred yards.

Around the same time during the Civil War, American physician Richard Gatling invented the gun that is named after him. The Gatling gun was often mounted on a wheeled carriage and avoided the Agar gun's overheating problems by having revolving multiple barrels. The gun was first used in 1864 during the Union siege of Petersburg. Gatling built the gun with ten barrels firing 400 .30-caliber bullets per minute. The U.S. Army adopted the gun and it remained in use for the next forty years. During the Indian Wars in the American West, the Gatling gun gave small numbers of U.S. cavalrymen a fighting chance against superior Native American forces.

The Gatling gun itself may have been made obsolete in the early 1900s, but its design was resurrected recently for use in the Vulcan minigun, which fires 6,000 rounds per minute. Mounted on helicopters and flying gunships, the guns saved the lives of many Americans in Vietnam. More recently, with the creation of the Fairchild Republic A-10 Warthog, Gatling's design of multiple revolving barrels is put on display as devastatingly effective. The A-10 was built around the 7-barrel GAU-8 Avenger. Powered by the plane's engine hydraulics, it fires 30mm spent uranium bullets at 4,200 rounds per minute. A single barrel wouldn't last long under this tremendous rate of fire, but Gatling's invention is still being used on today's battlefield.

The First True Machine Gun

British inventor Sir Hiram Maxim created the first modern machine gun in 1884. Instead of requiring a person to mechanically advance a new cartridge into the chamber, the Maxim machine gun used recoil from the previous shot to move the bolt to the rear, while a new cartridge moved in front of the bolt. Then, when the bolt, operated by a spring, returned forward, it pushed the new cartridge into the chamber. Using gas from fired cartridges helped heat escape from the barrel, which allowed the barrel to remain at a cooler temperature than previous weapons. The Maxim was a successful machine gun—it fired 600 rounds per minute—but it was heavy and required a team of men to operate.

A few years later, American gun maker legend John Moses Browning designed the M1917 Browning machine gun that U.S. forces used for the next several decades, through both World Wars, Korea, and Vietnam. Fed with ammunition belts and cooled with a water jacket around the barrel, the gun's rate of fire varied from 450 to 600 rounds per minute. Firing the then-standard .30-06 cartridge, the gun ejected spent casings from the bottom instead of the side. To save weight and for a simpler design, the weapon used a sliding block locking bolt. Still, the gun was very heavy at just under 140 pounds, but it was just as reliable. In military trials the gun fired continuously for more than 48 minutes without a malfunction.

Near the end of World War I, Browning designed the M2, a heavy .50-caliber machine gun that's still in use today. Like the lighter Browning machine gun, the M2 is air-cooled and belt-fed. Browning designed not only the weapon, but also the .50 BMG cartridge. BMG stands for Browning machine gun, and the round is used by the modern U.S. military as an anti-material and long-range anti-personnel round. Browning designed the gun to fire the larger bullet because aircraft were using heavier armor and the U.S. wanted machine guns that were effective against armored vehicles and planes.

Newer machine guns, specifically the M60, have gained popularity because of their rate of fire and reliability, as well as being lightweight. But these modern weapons got their start in the dusty pages of history, where inventors worked tirelessly to construct quality weapons. The descendants of those early weapons now have become common on the battlefield and have become the trusty companions of every fighting man and woman the world over.

Gatling Gun

The most famous of Richard Gatling's inventions, the Gatling gun, had its origins in pistols some 300 years earlier. Named pepperbox pistols because of their resemblance to a pepper mill, these multi-barrel pistols were crudely made and fired with matchlock. When the simpler and more reliable flintlock replaced the matchlock, pepperbox pistols were commonly fired with one hammer, which held the sharp piece of flint, and each barrel had its own hardened steel frizzen. After each shot, the shooter manually rotated the next barrel to the top of the pistol, making it ready to fire again. Pepperboxes made after the 1830s rotated the barrels as the hammer was cocked, just like a modern-day single-action revolver.

These pistols were heavy because of the multiple barrels and were difficult to aim because they didn't have sights. Without sights, the guns couldn't be aimed accurately and with their smoothbore barrels, the guns weren't good for targets past 20 feet. Deciphering who made the first pepperbox pistol is difficult because no European filed for a patent. English gun maker Henry Nock made several pepperbox pistols in the late 1700s and in Massachusetts and Rhode Island, Benjamin and Barton Darling filed a patent in 1836.

The next year, Massachusetts gun maker Ethan Allen obsoleted the Darlings' pistol when he patented a double-action pepperbox. On this pistol, pulling the trigger cocked the hammer, rotated the barrels, and fired the gun. Most pepperboxes were mass-produced and boasted four or six barrels. Allen's double-action pistol didn't need a big spur on the hammer to give the shooter's thumb enough purchase to cock the gun. Instead, the flat hammer allowed the pistol to be made sleek enough to slide into coat pockets for protection.

Colt's Revolver

In 1836 Samuel Colt patented the revolver, which sped the decline of the heavy pepperbox. The pepperbox survives today in the form of Heckler & Koch's battery-powered P11 underwater pistol. Made in Paterson, New Jersey, the Colt Paterson used a revolving cylinder and one stationary barrel. Unlike later revolvers, the Colt Paterson didn't include a loading rod, so after shooting all five shots, the shooter had to completely remove the cylinder from the gun to reload.

There were several improvements made to the revolver, but the biggest change came as brass cartridges gained popularity. Until that point, revolvers used a percussion cap on each cylinder, and then the shooter loaded the cylinders with powder and a lead ball. In the 1850s, Smith and Wesson made the first revolvers to fire cartridges. Their pistol had a hinge in front of the cylinder that allowed a shooter to open up the pistol and expose the back of the cylinder for reloading. Another design allowed the cylinder to swing out away from the pistol frame.

The final development for the revolver came in 1851 when English gun maker Robert Adams patented the double-action revolver, which used a long trigger pull to rotate the cylinder, cock the hammer, and fire the gun, like the Ethan Allen pepperbox.

Artillery Advancements

During advancements in pistol technology, similar advancements were being made in artillery. Wilson Agar designed an artillery piece that rapidly fired the .58-caliber cartridges also shot by rifled infantry muskets. The Agar gun had a single barrel that heated up and required a crew of men to load. These factors combined to limit the gun's rate of fire to 120 rounds per minute. A big drawback to the Agar gun was its tight tolerances, which made it ill equipped to handle the dirt and grime encountered in a combat role.

Enter Richard Gatling, who was born in North Carolina the son of a planter and inventor. Richard took after his father and in addition to his famous gun, he also patented a rice seed planter and a wheat drill. Gatling's first invention was a propulsion screw for steam ships, but when he tried to file his patent, he discovered that the same design had recently been patented. He succeeded in designing and patenting a double-hemp break, a steam tractor, a steam-powered ram, a gunmetal alloy, and a motorized tractor.

There are many theories as to why Gatling turned his attention from his other inventions toward guns. Gatling was wealthy at the start of the Civil War and wrote to Samuel Colt's niece that he invented the gun so it would do the work of a hundred soldiers, reducing the size of armies and thus minimizing soldiers' exposure to disease. He also wrote to President Abraham Lincoln that he hoped his gun would help the North crush the southern rebels in short order.

Gatling's Gun

He patented his artillery piece in 1862. Like a pepperbox, Gatling's gun had six barrels, and like a double-action revolver, the barrels rotated with a mechanism. In this case, a hand crank rotated the barrels and fired the gun. Gravity dropped the paper cartridges incased in steel chambers from a hopper into the barrels. The gun fired 600 rounds per minute and by spreading the load across six barrels, they stayed cool enough that overheating wasn't a concern. Using multiple barrels also reduced bore erosion in the barrels, which had been a problem in earlier rapid-firing guns.

But the gun wasn't perfect. Its chambers didn't always align with the barrels, hurting its accuracy and velocity. The system of placing paper cartridges into steel tubes before loading was time-consuming and required a team of crewmen. And its bizarre looks didn't win any fans either. There were also unfounded rumors of Gatling's involvement with a group of Confederate sympathizers even as he tried to sell his invention to the Union.

Because of these downfalls, the U.S. Ordnance Department didn't buy any and the Gatling gun saw very little use in the Civil War. But several Union generals, including Winfield Scott Hancock, Benjamin Butler, and David Porter, purchased guns for $1,000 each with their own money, but the gun saw actual combat only once, at Petersburg. It wasn't until 1866, after Gatling refined the gun to allow it to shoot metallic cartridges, that the U.S. Army adopted it.

Although the Gatling gun wasn't introduced in time or in large enough quantity to change the outcome of the Civil War, it was a big step in firearms technology. Before the Gatling gun, there were volley-firing weapons, such as the mitrailleuse gun, but even though these weapons fired a lot of projectiles in a short time, they had to be reloaded after each shot and it was a time-consuming task. This meant that while firing was quick, the continuous rate of fire was slow.

Gatling's gun, because it allowed for reloading while it was shooting, didn't have a reloading lag. And while it took a while for the American military to catch onto the Gatling, the gun was a major player in conflicts around the world for the next 40 years, until the first true machine appeared.

Around the World

Russia started buying Gatling guns in 1862 and more Gatlings were built in Russia than in any other country. Some of these guns were enlisted in World War II to help protect Russia's border with China. Gatling guns were mounted on camels in Egypt, Afghanistan, and Persia. In Africa and the Sudan the British used Gatling guns and during the Zulu War, 13 British soldiers used two Gatling guns to kill 500 Zulu warriors. In the Sudan, British soldiers were able to repel large-scale attacks.

After the American Civil War, the U.S. government used Gatling guns in the West during the Indian wars and there were 494 Gatling Guns in use throughout the U.S. military by 1895. The weapon's greatest hour in combat with American forces came in the Spanish-American War during the Battle of Santiago in Cuba. Three Gatling guns fired 18,000 rounds in less than eight minutes and saved many Americans. General George Custer decided against bringing Gatling guns with his cavalry force when they rode to their doom in 1876. Historians have long debated whether Gatling guns would have changed the battle's outcome.

Modern Improvements

At the end of World War II, thoughts returned to when Gatling had hooked up his gun to an electric power source. The U.S. Army contracted with General Electric in 1946 for Project Vulcan, which resulted in a rotating six-barrel cannon that fired 20mm shells at 4,000 rounds per minute. Many jets, including the F-18 Hornet and F-22 Raptor, use these cannons.

While most modern planes use their guns as secondary weapons after missiles, the A-10 Thunderbolt was literally designed around its huge 30mm Avenger rotating-barrel cannon. The gun system is placed on the plane's left side because the barrels fire when in the 9 o' clock position. With the firing barrel directly on the plane's center line, the gun's recoil doesn't change the plane's direction. Accurate enough to place 80 percent of its shots within a 40-foot circle, and powered by hydraulics from the plane's engines, the gun's main ammunition is armor-piercing rounds made of depleted uranium. Including its ammunition and feed system, the Avenger weighs in at 20 tons.

One hundred years after Gatling's most famous invention, his design has proven to be versatile enough to have its firepower increased from 660 rounds per minute to 4,000. The design was a good one. American ground troops who call in ground support from A-10s can thank Richard Gatling for the fast-shooting and hard-hitting rotating-barrel gun.

Mitrailleuse Gun

Historians aren't clear on the genesis of the
Mitrailleuse gun. Most agree that Belgian
Toussaint-Henry-Joseph Fafchamps designed
the first gun of this kind, which was then
produced by gun maker Joseph Montigny in
1860. Montigny, hoping to land a military
contract, then presented the gun to Napoleon III,
who had written books speculating about the
future of artillery. The French military had
recently begun using a small 4-pounder rifled
cannon, which were more accurate and had a
greater range than smoothbore cannons. But
these new rifled field pieces didn't shoot
grapeshot and canister (called "mitraille" by the
French) very well. With this change to rifled
cannons, the French forces found themselves in
need of anti-personnel artillery. This is where
Montigny's Mitrailleuse gun came in.

Artillery had been losing its advantage over small arms. At the time, rifling had increased the range of infantry muskets and their rate of fire had increased drastically while the range of cannons had increased only slightly and their rate of fire hadn't changed. The Mitrailleuse gun combined the musket's rate of fire and accuracy with the cannon's range and it achieved the same purpose as grapeshot but with greater range and accuracy, making it a perfect short-range companion for long-range rifled cannons.

Fafchamps' original gun fired from 50 barrels and used paper cartridges. He gave the gun the name "carabine multiple" and envisioned it as a stationary field gun for defending positions and fortifications. Montigny's improved artillery piece had 37 barrels and it was the prototype of the gun built in secret for the French for use in the Franco-Prussian War, which lasted from 1870 to 1871. It was the first rapid-firing gun mass-produced for use in combat. Still, only 210 of these second model Mitrailleuse guns were produced and their use stopped after the war. On the other side of the Atlantic, the Gatling gun was designed and it was used widely around the world and the design is still used for electric- and hydraulic-powered versions.

Napoleon III was sufficiently impressed with Montigny's design and he asked Jean-Baptiste Verchere de Reffye to work with Montigny to improve the design once more. The work was to be done in secret and to that end, the Reffye Mitrailleuse wasn't built in a single location: barrels were produced at one location, the breech at another, and the ammunition was made elsewhere. Word still got out and British newspapers reported that the French emperor was personally working on a new field gun. Only 200 copies of the gun were built for the start of the Franco-Prussian War.

How It Worked

Several countries built variations of the Mitrailleuse gun. They had different numbers of barrels that shot different caliber cartridges, but they all had a cluster of barrels and were usually mounted on wheeled carriages, bringing the total weight of the gun and carriage to about one ton.

A metal block holding the ammunition was locked against the gun's breech, holding the cartridges inside the chambers. A crank was then turned to fire the gun and the rate of fire depended on the turning speed. The large hand crank lent to the gun's nickname, the "coffee grinder." The gun's American counterpart, the Agar gun, had a similar nickname — the coffee mill gun. On the Mitrailleuse gun, every barrel had its own firing pin that was under spring pressure toward the gun's muzzle. The firing pins were held back from the cartridges' primers by a metal plate with channels and holes cut into it. When the crank turned, this plate moved horizontally. The holes were cut in such a way that as the plate moved, one firing pin would spring forward and fire its cartridge, then another pin would be released to fire, and so on. It was a primitive system, but it worked.

After the ammunition was fired, the ammunition plate was removed from the gun and a loaded plate replaced it and was locked into the breech. The loading and firing process were manual processes, unlike in the Gatling gun, whose loading just required pouring cartridges into a feeding magazine. The advancement of the Mitrailleuse was that it was much faster to load when compared to muskets and artillery of the day. Because the loading process was a manual one, its rate of fire was wholly dependent on the capability of its crew. A skilled artillery crew would use a Mitrailleuse to fire four 25-round volleys per minute. Three cartridge blocks were kept in a cycle — one was in the gun being fired, one was being loaded, and the cartridges were being pressed into the third.

A New Cartridge

In addition to firing quickly, the Mitrailleuse launched a powerful 13mm cartridge, which was the most advanced projectile of the day. The cartridge was similar to a modern shotgun shell with a rolled brass base with a rim topped with a stiff cardboard or tin body, which contained the powder charge of 185 grains of compressed black powder and a 770-grain paper patched bullet. The bullet developed 1,560 feet per second of velocity at the muzzle, which was faster than the lighter weight musket Minié balls. This fast-moving heavy bullet produced tremendous energy and penetrating force, which wouldn't be matched for another 20 years when smokeless powder was invented. The Mitrailleuse's projectiles reached out to 1,800 yards, well beyond the range of muskets.

Unfortunately for the French, these new guns weren't used to support infantry, but replaced cannon as artillery pieces and were typically fielded in batteries of six. Prussian artillery pieces had an effective range of 2,500 yards, which was about 700 yards more than the Mitrailleuse. Prussian artillery crews used this range advantage and usually destroyed the French gun crews while they weren't able to return fire. This was exactly the situation during a battle in August 1870. A French Mitrailleuse unit positioned their guns on an open hill. Prussian artillery crews destroyed Mitrailleuse ammunition supplies and killed one of the French artillery commanders, before the Mitrailleuse crews retreated. Later that month, the French used the new gun to support infantry. They positioned Mitrailleuse guns in woods on the flank of French infantry and this proved to be tremendously effective. The gun crews were hidden from Prussian artillery while they decimated Prussian infantry who were moving across an open field.

Instead of excelling at close range shooting, the Mitrailleuse guns were mostly used for distant targets. The Mitrailleuse could be swept horizontally left and right with a crank to create sweeping fire, but the gun couldn't turn wide enough. This created a very narrow path of fire and the sweep wasn't fast enough to be effective against enemy soldiers at close range and several times, soldiers were shot with multiple bullets. According to reports, one Prussian officer was killed when he was struck by four bullets fired from a Mitrailleuse gun 650 yards away. French soldiers tried to solve this problem by creating cartridges capable of firing multiple projectiles for close-range shooting, but the idea wasn't feasible for use in the gun's rifled barrels.

Historical Impact

The first machine gun to be used in combat, the Mitrailleuse's historical significance is questionable. We know it could have been more effective had it been used differently. The gun and its soldiers would have served better if, rather than being used as artillery, they supported the flanks of infantry units. That would have allowed the infantry to protect the Mitrailleuse and the Mitrailleuse to repel charges, killing 25 enemy soldiers at a time. It wasn't the super weapon the French had hoped it would be. Like the Nazis' rocket-powered bombs and jet airplanes showed, advanced technology is great, but unless leaders use it wisely, it'll only be recorded in history books as interesting footnotes and "what-ifs."

But the technology was new to military leaders and they were learning how to best use the Mitrailleuse. The gun inflicted terrible casualties and in addition to its quantifiable casualties, historians also consider the psychological factor of the gun's powerful cartridge and speedy rate of fire. And historians point out that Prussian artillery often concentrated their fire on the Mitrailleuse units and away from infantry and other artillery.

The end of the Franco-Prussian War also marked the end of the Mitrailleuse gun and it was moved from fighting on the front lines to fighting on the edges of France's empire. It earned the dubious honor of being the shortest-lived rapid-fire gun used in battle. After the Franco-Prussian War, the Mitrailleuse gun was used mostly for defending fortified positions. France's bad experience with the Mitrailleuse made the country hesitant to develop a better rapid-fire gun. Germany, who had been on the business end of the French's gun, realized its potential and set about creating a better version. Likewise, England wanted to build a machine gun and in the 1880s British inventor Hiram Maxim designed the world's first true machine gun, which changed warfare tactics once more. The new gun was lighter, boasted a much faster rate of fire, and was automated, needing only a small crew to operate. Today, the only remaining part of the Mitrailleuse gun still in use is its name. The word "mitrailleuse" has become the general French term for "machine gun."

Handgun

Soon after the invention of guns, some military officers wanted to make them as big as possible to hurl massive projectiles against fortifications. Others wanted to create small, handheld weapons that could quickly be stuffed into a bag or belt. Originally introduced in the 1500s, early matchlock and wheelock pistols were made in Europe, but weren't popular because their size and weight made them impractical. These early handguns were called pistols after the French word "pistolet."

The invention in the late 1600s of the flintlock ignition system enabled gun makers to create smaller and lighter pistols. The first of these successful handguns was known as the Queen Anne pistol because it gained popularity in England during her reign in the early 1700s. These pistols were unique because they loaded from the breech while all other guns at the time and most firearms made through the next 100 years loaded from the muzzle. The pistol consisted of a curved wooden grip that resembled the handle of a walking cane, a flintlock, and a tapered barrel, most of which were rifled. The barrel was threaded at the breech where it attached to the grip. After firing a shot, the shooter would twist off the barrel and load a ball and black powder, then screw the barrel back onto the pistol. The barrel's rifling held the slightly oversized ball from rolling out the muzzle. After priming the flintlock pan with fine black powder, the pistol was ready to shoot. The large ball tightly gripped the rifling and sealed in the expanding gases of the exploding powder charge. This not only gave the Queen Anne pistol accuracy, but also better muzzle velocity than smoothbores.

Military pistols were usually fully stocked with wood, meaning that the wooden grip extended for most of the length of the barrel and most pistols were smoothbore. Short barrels couldn't shoot undersized balls accurately at all and at ranges past 15 feet, an officer wielding a pistol may do better to throw the pistol at his enemy. Not all pistols were this futile, though. Some transplanted German gunsmiths living in Pennsylvania were building handguns as well as longrifles. Like their legendary rifle counterparts, most of these pistols had rifled barrels. Loaded from the muzzle, they used cloth patches and soft lead balls that were just smaller than the barrels' bores. When fired, the patch and tightly fitting ball would form a gas seal and similar to the Queen Anne pistol, these pistols shot with greater range and accuracy than their smoothbore counterparts. A good shooter could hit a 10-inch circle at 20 paces eight times out of 10.

Pistols caught on only where having a small lightweight gun was more important than having an accurate one. They never gained much traction on the American frontier, where the smoothbore fowler and Pennsylvania longrifle were much more practical. Pirates and sailors often used pistols tucked in their belts when boarding a ship. The infamous pirate Blackbeard was known to carry four Queen Anne pistols. With single-shot weapons, the way to gain more firepower was simply to carry more guns.

Pocket Guns

The invention of percussion locks allowed pistols to be even smaller and more streamlined. The smallest of these early pocket pistols was the Deringer, made by Henry Deringer in Philadelphia. Deringer made about 15,000 pistols, most in matching pairs, as they were very popular with city dwellers who wanted protection on dark streets. Most of Deringer's pistols were a hefty .41-caliber and stocked in walnut. The Philadelphia Deringer will remain famous for its use by John Wilkes Booth in the assassination of President Abraham Lincoln in 1865.

Deringers remained widely used until the invention of the revolver, which stretched a small gun's firepower to five or six shots instead of only one. The small single-shot pistol did make one notable comeback during the Second World War. The United States built the M1942 Liberator .45-caliber pistol. Designed in 1942 to be cheaply mass-produced, the pistol was intended to be air-dropped over occupied Europe to arm resistance forces. The small pistol was easy to produce as most of its 23 parts were stamped. To make the pistol easy to use, it was packaged in a cardboard box with illustrated instructions, 10 rounds, and a wooden dowel to push the spent cartridge out of the smoothbore barrel. The thinking behind the gun's manufacture was that citizens would find the guns and sneak up behind a solitary German soldier, kill him, and steal his weapon. The Liberators cost about $30 in modern currency and took only 7 seconds to build, making them faster to build than to load.

In the early 1800s, the pepperbox pistol replaced the Deringer as the pocketable pistol of choice for the simple reason that the pepperbox could hold four or six shots before needing to be reloaded. Most pepperbox pistols used a percussion ignition system. This allowed the guns to be slimmer than their flintlock predecessors. The pistols used four or six rotating smoothbore barrels. Early pepperbox pistols required the shooter to manually turn the barrels after each shot and later pistols used a double-action trigger, where the trigger rotated the barrels, drew the hammer, and fired the pistol. Because they weren't accurate, these pistols didn't wear sights. They were bulky and very muzzle-heavy because of the heavy barrels.

The Revolver

Samuel Colt solved this problem when he created the Colt Paterson in 1836. Instead of having multiple barrels, Colt's pistol, the first successful revolver, used a rotating cylinder and a single barrel. The cylinder held the powder and projectile for five shots. Before each shot, the shooter cocked the hammer to make the gun ready to fire. Because the trigger performed only one function—to release the hammer to fire the gun—this is called a single-action revolver. These pistols were also given the name "cap and ball" because their cylinders had a cap, powder charge, and lead ball for each shot. Smith and Wesson built the first revolver to use the new brass cartridges in the 1850s, but most Civil War generals and soldiers used cap and ball pistols. A few years after the war, in 1873, Colt created a legendary revolver, the Single Action Army, commonly called the Peacemaker or the Gun that Won the West. It was a single-action, six-shot .45-caliber and it was made in several variations until 1941.

English gun maker Robert Adams patented the double-action revolver in 1851, but the single-action pistol remained trusted in America until the 1870s when Colt and Smith and Wesson began making double-actions. With this type of pistol, the trigger rotates the cylinder, draws back the hammer, and releases it to fire the gun. The double-action revolver was improved over the next 20 years and it became the trusted sidearm of many American police forces, but the military switched to a new and advanced pistol design.

Semi-Automatic Pistols

Across the Atlantic, German gun maker Georg Luger was designing a pistol that would forever be linked to Nazi Germany. In 1898 Luger patented his toggle-locked semi-automatic pistol and production began a few years later. Luger also designed a new cartridge, the 9mm. The toggle was on top of the pistol and folded up in the middle like a knee joint. When in firing position, it was overextended and pushed the cartridge into the chamber. The pistol was reliable and heavily sought-after by American GIs in both World Wars. American gun maker William Ruger designed his first firearm, the Mark 1 .22 automatic pistol, after the Luger to the extent that Ruger's gun is nicknamed the Ruger Luger.

Legendary American gun maker John Moses Browning was working on a semi-automatic pistol of his own. In the early 1900s, he designed some successful prototypes that were manufactured and became popular. One of these was the 1903 Pocket Hammerless, chambered for .32 ACP and .38 ACP, which Browning also designed. Outlaws Bonnie and Clyde carried the Hammerless as did Al Capone. John Dillinger was drawing a Hammerless to fire on FBI agents when he was killed.

But Browning wasn't content to stop at his 1903 gun, which fired low-powered cartridges, and in 1911, he created an American masterpiece, the M1911 .45 ACP. The gun has been known since then as simply "the 1911." American soldiers carried the 1911 into battle for the next 60 years, through the Vietnam War. Because of its reliability, some U.S. military units still carry the 1911 even though it has been largely phased out by the Beretta M9. The 1911 is still popular with American citizens and it appears regularly in several shooting competitions.

It seemed like nothing would dethrone the 1911, but in 1982 Austrian Gaston Glock began producing the Glock 17, a polymer-framed 9mm. Although it was originally greeted with skepticism because of its plastic components, the Glock pistol has joined the 1911 as the gold standard of pistol reliability. Most gun companies have copied the Glock design and polymer pistols have now replaced every other type of pistol in a majority of American police forces.

As more Americans decide to exercise their Second Amendment rights and choose to legally carry a firearm, the market for small guns has greatly expanded in the past five years. Polymer pistols, because of their light weight, have become the most popular choices. Henry Deringer might be proud to see that we never abandoned his idea — Americans still use small guns to protect themselves. It's just that now, those guns look a little different.

Autocannon

Automatic cannons are rapid-fire artillery pieces that fire a variety of large shells. The biggest difference between machine guns and autocannons is the ammunition they shoot. Whereas machine guns typically fire bullets that are .50-caliber or smaller, autocannons shoot explosive shells and armor-piercing rounds that are 20mm or larger. Autocannons were originally used as artillery pieces, but as technology has improved, they are used on airplanes, naval ships, and armored vehicles, and they also serve as antiaircraft guns.

Englishman Hiram Maxim invented his machine gun in 1884 and a few years later, he designed the QF 1-pounder, often called the Pom-pom. It was basically a scaled-up version of his machine gun as it fired 37mm explosive shells at 200 rounds per minute. It was a revolutionary weapon for its time—it increased artillery's rate of fire and range. Maxim's own country didn't purchase any of the guns at first, but many other countries—including the South African Republic, which was fighting the British in the Boer War—did. As British forces discovered the effectiveness of Maxim's gun from being on the wrong end of it, they demanded some of the guns.

Since its shell was too small for use as an infantry weapon and it was too weak for use against fortifications, the QF was used by the British military in an anti-aircraft role in the First World War. But while defending Britain, the gun quickly showed its weakness against the German's new weapon, the Zeppelin. The 37mm shell wasn't able to make explosions large enough to bring down these airships. One British gunner in 1914 needed 75 rounds to bring down a Zeppelin. The gun was mounted on aircraft to determine its feasibility, but it was replaced quickly with other, lighter guns. The QF design was improved into a two-pounder, which served as both anti-aircraft artillery and as a close-range weapon for naval ships.

Revolver Cannon

Like the machine gun, the autocannon's family tree begins with the flintlock Puckle gun, invented in 1718. It was followed by the mitrailleuse and Agar guns and the much more successful Gatling gun, patented in 1862. But these weapons were rapid fire guns—they fired bullets, not explosive shells. Some autocannons can trace their genealogy to Samuel Colt's successful revolver, patented in 1836. Revolver cannons, like Colt's pistol, use rotating cylinders that hold shells. Other autocannons are more directly descended from machine guns because the artillery pieces use belt- or magazine-fed ammunition.

German Anton Politzer was the first to create a successful revolver cannon—the MG 213, which fired a 330-grain 30mm shell at about 1,740 feet per second. Developed toward the end of World War II, the gun was envisioned as an airplane-mounted cannon for special use against armored bombers and as a bomber defense anti-aircraft gun. Unfortunately for the Luftwaffe, the gun was designed too late to do any good and only 10 were built before the war ended.

While the gun did little to help the Nazis, the French, British, and Americans all copied the gun and improved its design. Improved versions of Politzer's design have become the standard cannon in many European fighter planes, and Britain's ADEN cannon, France's DEFA cannon, and America's M39 cannon all trace their roots to the World War II design.

These revolver autocannons usually have a lower rate of fire than multi-barrel Gatling-style autocannons. At operating speed, Gatling-style cannons can fire up to 10,000 rounds per minute, but revolver-style cannons can fire only about 2,000 rounds in the same time. Revolver autocannon barrels also heat up much quicker than do multi-barrel cannons. But when the initial start-up rates of fire are compared, the revolver cannon fires faster because it has much less metal mass to spin than a Gatling-style cannon that fires the same size shell.

The Prolific Oerlikon

The other type of autocannon uses one barrel and a belt or magazine feed. This type of cannon was pioneered during the First World War by German Reinhold Becker when he created a 20mm cannon known simply as the 20mm Becker. The cannon fired at 300 rounds per minute and was used very sparsely on aircraft and as an anti-aircraft gun. When the war came to an end, the Treaty of Versailles forbade the production of the autocannon by Germany, so in 1919, a Swiss gun manufacturer purchased the patents and continued to improve the weapon. By 1924, an improved Becker cannon fired an improved cartridge — one that launched heavier rounds at a higher rate of fire.

In 1924 the Oerlikon Company took over the Swiss firm and three years later, the company had created a still larger gun that fired a larger cartridge, with the goal of using the gun against tanks and aircraft. Both the Allied and Axis forces used variations of the Oerlikon cannon during World War II and many of today's autocannons trace their lineage to the Oerlikon.

The Oerlikon uses a simple blowback system to work its bolt. Rather than locking into the barrel breech just before firing, a blowback cannon moves freely to rest against the rear of the cartridge. When the shell is fired, the recoil or blowback forces the bolt backwards. A heavy spring stops the bolt's rearward movement and forces it forward again, shoving another shell into the chamber. This method of using the shell's recoil to cycle the bolt greatly reduces the cannon's felt recoil. The cannon's long chamber necessitated a special shell to be custom made. The shell cartridge has a short neck, straight sides, and a rebated rim, meaning the cartridge rim or base is smaller in diameter than the shell itself. This allows the extractor claws to grab the cartridge while it is in the chamber and remove it, making space for the next shell. To make the extractor's job easier, early cartridges were greased, but during World War II, grooves were cut into the chamber walls to ease extraction.

Ammunition was fed by a 60-round drum magazine on top of the cannon. Belt-fed variations of the cannon were designed to overcome the limiting factor of frequent magazine changes. Other versions of the Oerlikon cannon were designed and built to adapt the weapon to different applications. For naval ships, the cannon was mounted on a pedestal and had a steel shield to protect the gun's crew. The gunner used a belt and shoulder supports to attach himself to the gun, which he aimed with the basic spider-web and bead sighting. The gun was also mounted with two- and four-barrel configurations on British and American ships and smaller patrol boats. And last, the cannon's manufacturer designed a variation to fit it to the wings of aircraft. There were three minor variations of these cannons that fired different 20mm shells of different weights. The cannons firing the smaller shells had a greater rate of fire, reaching 520 rounds per minute. This was the feared gun that gave the Messerschmitt Bf 109 its teeth. In the Pacific theater, a Japanese version of the Oerlikon cannon made the Mitsubishi A6M Zero a formidable opponent.

American naval ships used Oerlikon-type cannons to replace its M2 Browning machine guns because the cannons had a much longer range and the exploding 20mm shell carried much more destructive force than a .50-caliber bullet. Ships mainly used the cannon to protect against aircraft, but was eventually replaced by 40mm and 3-inch guns, whose shells were more effective at stopping kamikaze planes. The Canadian Navy also used the Oerlikon gun against ships with light armor and against submarines that wore thin steel skin. The cannon was also used as the basis for arming small British tanks in World War II. Today's use of the gun is mostly limited to ships to fire warning shots or for use as a last-resort weapon.

Today's Autocannons

While today's autocannons have very fast rates of fire, they don't often run at full speed. Most of these cannons would overheat with sustained fire and would quickly run out of ammunition if their speed were not governed. Some autocannons are limited to 90 rounds per minute because planes and vehicles can carry only so much ammunition. Airplane-mounted cannons typically use a higher rate of fire, reaching 10,000 rounds per minute, because with both the target and the shooter moving, the gun has less time on the target than do vehicle-mounted guns. Plane-mounted guns are typically fired in short bursts because of this short time on target.

As guided missiles entered the scene in the mid-1950s, they reduced the reliance on autocannons, but didn't entirely replace them. American pilots realized during the Vietnam that autocannons could be used sometimes to save a much more expensive missile. America's M3 Bradley armored vehicle uses the 25mm electric rotary cannon called the M242 Bushmaster. Unlike earlier autocannons, the Bushmaster uses a motor to feed ammunition, fire, and extract shells. It uses gears rather than recoil or gases to cycle the bolt. This system allows the gunner to quickly switch the type of ammunition he shoots. He can choose from a range of penetrating or explosive shells—a dream come true for those British soldiers trying to shoot down Zeppelins that threatened to rain down bombs on England.

Artillery Gun

The earliest forms of artillery were siege engines that slung massive arrows, stones, diseased animals, and flaming projectiles over fortress walls or into a crowd of enemy infantry. Roman Legions used these large artillery pieces, which used torque and leverage, before 1 A.D. The machines weren't efficient with their energy and so the invention of gunpowder brought major changes.

When gunpowder started being used in the 1100s, artillery joined primitive shoulder-fired weapons. The word "artillery" comes from the French "atelier," meaning to arrange, and the Italian "arte de tirare," or the art of shooting. The word was used to refer to those who built weapons, but later it came to refer to guns—cannons, mortars, and howitzers. And though they may have started out as primitive weapons, artillery has become one of war's deadliest weapons, accounting for half of the battlefield deaths between the 1750s and 1850s and most of the combat deaths during the Napoleonic Wars and both World Wars.

Early Examples

Song Dynasty General Han Shizhond used early bronze cannons called huochond during a battle in 1132 and German military leader Johann Ziska used gunpowder artillery pieces in warfare during the Hussite Revolution from 1419 to 1434. These early artillery pieces weren't large tubes, but were staves of metal banded together, like a cooper's wooden barrel. Some historians say this is where the gun's "barrel" got its name. The first artillery pieces were huge and heavy, making them un-maneuverable and susceptible to a rapidly advancing enemy. As shoulder-fired firearms grew in popularity and became smaller and more manageable, so did artillery pieces.

As metalworking technology advanced, cannons were made of single solid pieces of iron or bronze cast around a core, which created the bore. The earliest record of a drilled bore comes from 1247 in Spain. These huge smoothbore weapons could fire a number of projectiles, ranging from forged iron balls to rocks, but their size and weight limited their mobility. For the next several hundred years, cannons were increasingly made of iron and were made smaller and more maneuverable by being placed on wheeled carriages. The only significant advancement during this time was the ammunition these guns shot. They shot solid iron balls, of course, but gunners also used canister, grapeshot, bar shot, and chain shot. Canister and grapeshot essentially turned cannons into huge powerful shotguns and made them very effective against infantry by shooting a cluster of iron balls. Bar shot and chain shot were used by seamen to cut down the masts and rigging of enemy ships. Bar show was a cannonball cut with the two halves connected with a five-inch iron bar. Chain shot was the ball cut in two with a chain connecting the halves. These guns were muzzleloaders and while a few attempts were made at creating breech loading cannons, the lack of strong enough materials and technical knowledge made these very dangerous with the breech end just as likely to cause harm as the muzzle end. James 2, King of Scots, who was a big proponent of artillery, was killed in 1460 when a cannon exploded.

Use of the cannon was widespread. Both Portuguese and Moroccan armies used artillery in the early 1400s. The Hundred Year's War saw British forces use cannons against the Scottish and because the artillery pieces were powerful enough to reduce castles and stone fortifications to rubble, cannons were used in great number to defend and attack these walled defenses. Eventually, though, the cannon rendered castles obsolete as warfare defenses. French heroine Joan of Arc fought with and against artillery. In a battle in 1430, her forces attacked and defeated a fortification guarded by artillery. In other attacks, artillery units supported her forces' assaults and helped lead to her victories. Her attack against English-occupied Paris failed because of English artillery. Ottoman forces used several units of artillery to attack and defeat Constantinople in 1453. The famous Swedish military technician Gustavus Adolphus was an early champion of artillery who pushed for smaller and lighter cannons. Later, Napoleon, who was also champion of artillery and wrote several books about the cannon's use in warfare and the future of artillery, used massed artillery and he pioneered the strategy of pounding the enemy with a barrage to soften the target before an infantry or cavalry attack.

Artillery Advancements

In the 1600s artillery became more versatile with their ability to shoot explosives — a hollow iron ball filled with gunpowder and primed with a lit fuse. This gave rise to the mortar and howitzer. These big-bore guns had short barrels and were able to fire at high angles, allowing gunners to lob explosives over walls. The Russian military learned the mortar's usefulness during the Russo-Turkish War in the 1870s. During the Battle of Plewna, Turkish infantrymen took cover behind earthen defenses and weren't touched by Russian artillery. The artillery pieces couldn't tilt upward enough to drop shells onto the enemy infantry. Ten years later, Russia had a heavy field howitzer that was portable yet able to fire heavy projectiles.

It wasn't until the mid-1800s that rifling became common in cannon barrels and Claude-Étienne Minié's invention of the oblong pointed (conoidal) bullet, that artillery technology really experienced a breakthrough. Rifling gave cannons much greater range and accuracy, although it limited their ammunition to solid balls and conoidal shot. Stronger metals gave rise to breechloading cannons, which could be loaded to higher pressures than could muzzleloaders, which resulted in the projectiles traveling at higher velocities.

First 'Modern' Artillery

In 1855 Englishman William Armstrong designed the Armstrong gun, which was the foundational gun of modern artillery. The breechloaded gun's barrel was rifled and Armstrong designed a cast iron shell with a thin lead coating that was slightly larger than the bore. This made the lead swage into the rifle and spun the shell when it was fired. Armstrong also put a "grip" at the cannon's muzzle. Acting similar to a shotgun choke, the grip constricted the bore size to ensure the shell was centered in the barrel just before it left the muzzle. This stripped the lead shell coating and greatly improved the gun's accuracy. Another feature of the gun's design was how its construction allowed it to withstand high breech pressure. Rather than being cast from molten iron or hammer-forged, the Amrstrong gun's barrel was made of several thin tubes that built up thickness and increased the barrel's strength.

A few years before 1900, the French built another groundbreaking cannon. Called the French 75, the gun used a hydro-pneumatic piston to soak up recoil. This meant that the gun didn't move at all when it was fired. Gunners didn't need to reposition and re-aim the gun after each shot, which allowed for much faster follow-up shots. Because the gun used cartridge ammunition, reloading was fast with the breechloading gun. An experienced crew could fire 20 rounds each minute at targets five miles away.

New Strategies

With artillery's improved range came a new method of aiming. Indirect fire is the term given to shooting at a target that isn't visible from the artillery piece, whether the target is too far away or if it is behind a hill. The method uses a calculation of the shell's path to determine the angle it should be fired. The problem then became to find the enemy's position and get those coordinates to the gunners. The invention of aircraft in the early 1900s solved this problem. With the invention of radio communications came the firebase system of building artillery bases in positions where the guns can support infantry. In this scenario, infantry troops can radio to the firebase the enemy's locations and call for an artillery strike. This technique saved many American lives in World War II, Korea, and Vietnam.

Another new strategy came about during the trench warfare of the First World War. Called a creeping barrage, artillery would rain shells down immediately in front of its advancing soldiers. The barrage not only cleared the path for the foot soldiers, but also hid them in smoke from the enemy.

As advancements have allowed more explosives to fit into a small package, infantrymen carry small mortars and launching tubes. The tubes are smoothbore and for stabilization, the shells have fins that deploy when the shell leaves the muzzle. Modern artillery pieces fire a wide variety of shell types, including white phosphorus, nuclear, airburst, high-explosive, and shells that penetrate armor or hardened structures like concrete.

One more advancement has increased the destructive force of artillery. Studies show that the first 10 seconds of an artillery barrage are the most effective against personnel because people will not have taken cover in those early seconds. To take full advantage of this time, artillery uses the concept of "time of target." By adjusting the propellant of shells and by adjusting the angle of fire, multiple guns in different locations can fire several shells that will strike a target at the same time. Some guns have the ability to fire multiple rounds that hit the target simultaneously.

Tank Guns

Although there were many primitive attempts to build battle tanks, and despite the fact that Leonardo da Vinci designed one, the first real tanks appeared on the World War I battlefield. With the earlier invention of machine guns, the area between trenches, called No Man's Land, was a slaughterhouse where infantrymen would charge en masse and be cut down. Most of these charges failed to take any ground because there were so few soldiers who reached the enemy trenches.

The British army developed the first tank, appropriately name the Mark 1. The 28-ton vehicle moved at less than 4 miles per hour and carried two Hotchkiss 57mm QF guns and three .303 machine guns. The 6-pounder was an autocannon designed as a naval and coastal defense gun, but it was pressed into service for use on tanks. The Mark 1 and other early tanks were built primarily as troop movers, as transport vehicles to get soldiers across No Man's Land safely. For this reason, tank's guns were mostly used to defend the tank and the men inside. The QF guns' barrels were too long and they snagged on branches and barbed wire that littered the battlefield. Mounted in pods on the tank's sides, the cannons swiveled both vertically and horizontally, but their range of motion was still limited.

The British improved the tank's design a few times, giving the improved versions the designations Mark 2, Mark 3, and so on. The Mark 4 used the same 57mm gun, only with shorter barrels. This was the first gun built specifically for a tank. Germany's first tank, the A7V, was a huge machine that weighed in at 36 tons. A7Vs carried a 57mm Nordenfelt cannon and six machine guns. Tanks were first used in combat on April 1918 when 13 German tanks attacked British and Australian infantry at the battle of Villers Bretonneux. The world saw its first tank-versus-tank battle the following month in the same area when three British Mark 4 tanks took on a group of three German A7Vs. Most of the tanks were damaged and were abandoned. Germany built only 20 A7Vs during the war and so Allied tanks returned to their original role as troop carriers and infantry support.

First Modern Tank

The French joined the tank age in 1917 with the FT17 Renault. Built by the Renault car company, the FT17 moved slower than 5 miles per hour with its 39 horsepower crankstart engine and used a 37mm Puteaux breech-loading single-shot cannon for a main gun. While the gun was very reliable and not prone to jamming, its rate of fire was only 15 rounds per minute. The shell didn't develop much velocity and as a result, it wasn't able to penetrate thick armor and was used instead for lightly armored vehicles and pillboxes. The real feature that set this tank apart from early tanks was that the cannon was placed on a rotating turret. No longer would the entire tank need to line up with the cannon's target. The FT17 put all its trust in the cannon and didn't carry machine guns.

Since then, the cannon has become tanks' main weapon. Since those early tanks in World War I, tank cannons have grown more and more powerful, as they're able to fire armor-penetrating rounds, guided missiles, anti-aircraft rounds and high-explosive rounds. But early tanks used only adaptations of existing cannons and it wasn't until World War II that tank builders saw the necessity to design cannons just for tanks. Some tanks were designed to support infantry so they carried light guns and machine guns for attacking pillboxes and enemy soldiers. Another strategy of tank usage was to fight against enemy tanks. As newer tanks were designed to wear heavier armor, new guns were needed to fight against them. Unlike the early guns modified for tanks' usage, these new specially designed cannons could penetrate other tanks' thick armor.

Better Guns For Better Tanks

British light tanks used 37mm and 40mm cannons and even though these guns weren't effective against infantry, their small fast-moving projectiles were effective against thick armor. Like these light guns, the cannons built early on for use against other tanks weren't necessarily larger caliber cannons, but they fired small shells at high velocity, which gave them increased energy upon impact, giving them penetrating power.

As increasing tank armor quickly outpaced the penetrating ability of these guns, bigger and more powerful guns were designed for tanks. German's Panzer II tanks started the war with a 37mm cannon, then upgraded to a 50mm gun. The Panzer IV, Germany's main tank during the war, used the 75mm KwK 40 and Germany's last World War II tank, the Tiger, used an 88mm KwK 43, but few of these tanks were built in time to be effective for Germany's war effort.

Like the Germans, the Soviet Army produced tanks with increasingly powerful guns. The country's early T-34 and later KV-1 both used a 76.2 mm F-34 tank gun. The T-44 used 85-mm ZiS-S-53 tank gun. Although not many T-44s were produced, they served as the concept model for the T-54 and T-55, the most-produced tank in the world. The Soviets also designed the KV-2 tank, which used a howitzer to lob explosive shells over barriers and walls. Similarly, the British converted some of their tanks to carry howitzers, mainly the 94mm high explosive-firing gun.

In 1942, the American army fielded the Sherman tank. The tank wore two inches of armor, moved at 24 mph—just as fast as the Germans' Tiger—and used a 75mm cannon. The Tiger had a larger cannon, but because 5,000 Shermans were produced, compared with 2,000 Tigers, the Sherman had a larger impact on the battlefield. The American M5A1 Stuart tank was lighter and faster, moving at 36 mph. It was built as a scouting vehicle—small and maneuverable to get close to the enemy, look around, and get back to a safe area. The Stuart carried a 37mm gun, which was tiny compared to the larger tanks on the battlefield.

To combat the growing numbers of tanks, nations produced vehicles whose sole purpose was to fight against and destroy tanks. Most of these fast-moving vehicles were lightweight because they didn't carry much armor, but they did carry powerful cannons. America built the M18 Hellcat tank destroyer in 1944. Weighing only 20 tons, the Hellcat could reach 60 mph. Although it didn't carry much armor, the Hellcat's gun, a 76mm, was no lightweight. The tank destroyer entered the war at the Battle of the Bulge, where it demonstrated its tremendous maneuverability. It could run circles around the German's Tiger, which was more heavily armed and armored. The Hellcat's armor, though thin, was angled at a 45-degree angle to deflect shells. The German army used the idea and created its own Marder tank destroyer, which used a 76.2mm Russian field cannon and a Czechoslovakian tank frame.

Today's Tank Guns

As World War II ground to a stop, the winners and losers clearly evident, so too was the most popular choice of tank. Armies were building large battle tanks, rather than tank destroyers or small mobile tanks. As armor technology improved, well-protected tanks could also be lightweight, regardless of their large size. In an effort to defeat this armor and to make tanks a more effective battlefield weapon, their cannons grew in size and their ammunition improved. In the East, the 100mm cannon replaced the 85mm and now the 125mm cannon is the most typical. In 1960 the U.S. began producing the M60 Patton, a 53-ton tank that carried a 105mm gun, at the time outgunning the Russian T54' 100mm. Likewise, in other Allied countries, the popular 105mm became the 120mm.

As for ammunition, armor-piercing rounds and solid shot lacked penetrating force against new and improved armor. Instead, fin-stabilized rounds made of heavy tungsten and deplete uranium and penetrator rounds with discarding sabots, and high explosive rounds became common. Tank guns' aiming mechanisms also improved with technological advancements. Rangefinders and computer fire control systems account for wind and temperature to put rounds on the target.

While bore size and ammunition types have changed, tank guns themselves remain fairly similar to how they started, with rifled barrels. Rifling spins projectiles traveling down the barrel. This spin acts to stabilize and make the projectile fly more accurately, like a football when thrown in a tight spiral. With the advent of fin-stabilized projectiles, the barrel isn't needed to spin the projectile, and so some tanks are reverting to smoothbore cannons. A smoothbore barrel wears more slowly than a rifled version and the smooth bore accommodates a wider variety of shell types.

In 1985 the Abrams M1A1 tank burst upon the scene with a 120mm smoothbore cannon and the capability to move at 40 mph. With its fire control system able to hold the gun steady on target while the tank moves, the Abrams can fire eight rounds per minute and hit targets farther than two miles away. The Abram's bite comes from the main cannon, made by the German company, Rheinmetall. Like other tank cannons, the Abram's gun fires high explosive rounds, which use extremely hot gases that melt a hole in the side of an enemy tank's armor, and sabot-discarding penetrators. These shells use a narrow hard penetrating core. To center it in the barrel, a plastic sabot jackets the penetrator and then falls away once the shell exits the barrel, leaving the penetrator to breech enemy armor by simple force.

Hunting Guns

Since their invention, firearms have been used to kill game to put food on the table. A popular myth holds that when North America was first colonized by Westerners, the land that makes up modern-day America was so heavily wooded that a squirrel could travel from the Atlantic coast to the Mississippi River and never have to touch the ground. Game of all kinds was plentiful in the forest—squirrel and rabbit, duck and turkey, deer and bear. Early settlers came to the New World with heavy and cumbersome matchlocks. These guns often needed shooting sticks to make accurate shots because of their weight and slow ignition. The doglock replaced the matchlock. Doglocks were very similar to what would become flintlocks, except that a latch or "dog" on the outside of the lock plate held the hammer at half-cock during loading. As the shooter pulled the hammer to full-cock, the dog fell away and the internal mechanisms of the lock held the hammer in place until the gun was fired. The flintlock, with its internal tumbler notched at two spots, held the hammer at half-cock and obsoleted the doglock. In the 1720s, the British Army replaced its doglocks with flintlocks.

With the transition from matchlock to doglocks to flintlocks, firearms shrank and became more slender and lightweight. As metalworking advanced, barrels could be made with lower profiles and could be made lighter. Fowling guns were long and slender and the lightest of these early flintlocks. Built for shooting pieces of shot for birds, and buckshot and solid roundballs for larger game, these guns swung easily and the long barrel helped increase the constriction or "choke" when shooting shot. But with their smoothbore barrels, fowlers weren't well suited for shooting roundballs. For a single solid projectile, accuracy was limited to within 75 yards.

The Rifle

With the early 1700s, a major development dawned that has influenced every firearm made since then. Barrel makers discovered that by cutting a series of twisting grooves in a barrel, the grooves would impart spin on the roundball and make it fly straighter and farther than when the same projectile was fired from a smoothbore. Shooters took full advantage of this advancement by using tight patch-ball combinations. The thin cloth patch acted as a gasket to seal the gases behind the ball to ensure that no expanding gases slipped past the ball, and the patch also helped make the ball tight in the bore. Roundballs shot from a smoothbore fowler were generally loose-fitting to the bore and bounced around as they flew down the barrel, which increased their inaccuracy. Rifles used soft lead balls that were loaded so lightly that the patch texture was indented onto the ball during loading.

Flintlock rifles originated in Germany, where hunters, called jaegers, carried short large-caliber rifles. These rifles were ornately decorated with relief and incise carving, silver and gold inlays, and their expensive price tag reflected gunsmiths' craftsmanship. A rifle usually cost at least what a general laborer earned in a year. The German rifles themselves became known as jaegers. While fowlers had round barrels, rifles usually used octagonal barrels that were slightly heavier. Most jaegers used not straight-walled barrels but swamp barrels. These barrels had a consistent bore diameter, but had wide walls at the breech that then narrowed toward the muzzle and flared at the muzzle. This distribution of weight made the gun balance comfortably in the palm of the left hand for a right-handed shooter.

As German immigrants moved to America and settled throughout Pennsylvania, they brought with them the general styling of the jaeger to create the Pennsylvania longrifle. These guns were fancy and were longer, generally using barrels averaging 40 inches, and they were bored to shoot smaller caliber balls. A smaller caliber meant that less powder and lead, the supply of which was limited in the colonies, were needed for each shot. Flintlock rifles' accuracy allowed a skilled rifleman to hit an enemy soldier at 200 yards and there are reports from the American Revolution of American riflemen killing British officers at 300 yards. Flintlock muzzleloading rifles are popular in America for target matches and the farthest typical distance is 200 yards. At 100 yards, good shooters can put five shots in an eight-inch circle.

The flintlock was a major advancement in firing technology and it stayed active for more than one hundred years. One of the disadvantages of it and all previous technologies, the matchlock, snaplock, and wheel-lock, is its delay in firing. The lock lit some gunpowder in a firing pan located outside the barrel. The heat from the burning powder traveled into the barrel through a small touchhole.

Percussion Lock

In the early 1800s, Scottish minister Alexander Forsyth grew frustrated that while he was hunting ducks, the birds would flare off during the delay between the time his flintlock flashed in the pan and when the gun fired. He invented a cap filled with fulminate that exploded when struck with a hammer. The small cap set on the top of a nipple beside the barrel. When the trigger was pulled, the hammer fell on the cap, setting off the fulminate, which directed the tiny explosion through the nipple and into the barrel. Forsyth's invention didn't gain popularity until several years later and it replaced the flintlock. Unlike the flintlock, the percussion lock was more impervious to damp weather and it was faster to load.

The percussion or caplock gun gave more reliable ignition and it quickly gained popularity with hunters for whom a misfire meant a hungry family. Between 1815 and 1858 the St. Louis-based Jacob and Samuel Hawken made a name for themselves by making Plains rifles for mountain men and settlers heading west. These brave men needed reliable and rugged large-caliber rifles to kill buffalo, bear, elk, not to mention smaller animals for food and protection. Until metallic cartridges came into widespread use, the Hawken rifle and the Plains rifle were prized possessions across the American West.

Cartridges and Actions

Advancements in the late 1800s culminated in the metallic cartridge and new guns were designed to fire them. Whereas the percussion lock severely reduced the chances of a misfire and sped ignition, the metallic cartridge was virtually impervious to weather and produced rapid ignition. The shotgun shell also became popular during this time. The invention of these cartridges changed every gun that has been made since. Percussion guns were quickly exchanged for lever-action rifles and pump-action shotguns. Breech-loading rifles, such as the Sharps, the Spencer, and Remington's rolling block, were strong enough to handle powerful cartridges, such as the .50-120. The caliber designation signifies that the .50-caliber projectile was launched with 120 grains of black powder.

The invention of the rolling block saved Remington. When the Civil War ended, the U.S. government canceled its arms contracts with Remington. The company had hundreds of surplus guns that nobody wanted to buy because the war had already flooded the market with firearms. Instead of looking stateside for customers, Remington sold its rolling block to militaries in other countries, mostly in Europe. Still, the Remington remained a solid choice for American buffalo hunters because of its strong and simple action. In the rolling block design, an L-shaped breechblock pivoted against the back of the breech, and the exposed hammer was cocked by hand before each shot.

Remington's gun was only slightly less popular than the well-known Sharps rifle. The Sharps used a breechblock that operated with a pivoting trigger guard. As this metal loop was swung down, it pulled the breechblock downward, sliding in grooves, to expose the breech. Some Sharps rifles had double-set triggers. When the hammer was cocked and the gun was ready to fire, the shooter would pull the second trigger to "set" the front trigger, making it very light and easier to shoot accurately.

Hinge-action or break-open guns also grew in popularity, especially for shotguns. A lever is pushed and the gun hinges open to expose the breech. Most of these rifles and shotguns had two barrels, but some, called Drillings for the German word for "three," had three barrels. These guns had different combinations of shotgun and rifle barrels and were the ideal hunting firearm, capable of taking both large game and fowl. Most serious shotgun target shooters use over-under guns, with two vertically stacked barrels, which use the hinge action, and the famous double-barrel shotgun also uses this action, which makes it quick to load.

Bolt Action and Semiautomatic

The last two major developments in firearms brought about the modern hunting rifle and shotgun. In the late 1800s, the German Mauser company designed a strong bolt-action rifle, which the American Army quickly copied in 1903 to make its famous 1903 Springfield. Mauser's bolt-action was strong because it had three locking lugs that, when the bolt was rotated closed, tightened the action and readied it for firing. Previously, bolts had been made with only two lugs and they hadn't been strong enough to fire powerful cartridges. The 1903 Springfield was originally designed to fire the .30-03, but this round was found to be relatively weak when compared with other country's ammunition. Three years later, the .30-06 was designed and has since become America's most popular hunting cartridge, capable of taking any game animal in North America and most animals in Africa. Now the Remington 700 and Winchester Model 70, both bolt-actions, are America's favorite hunting rifles.

In the 1930s, interest grew in semi-automatic rifles and although the U.S. military's M1 Garand was arguably the best infantry weapon in the Second World War, the automatic rifle has never outpaced popularity among American hunters. But for shotgun hunters, the pump-action and semiautomatic guns are the most popular. The Remington 1100 is America's best-selling automatic, followed by those made by Mossberg, Beretta, and Benelli.

It's interesting to note that while bolt-actions are the popular hunting gun, some outdoorsmen are looking to get back to hunting's roots and the sport has come full circle as many hunters looking for a challenge head to the American West hoping to bag a trophy elk with a bow.

Ferguson Rifle

The first widely successful breechloading gun was the Queen Anne pistol, so named because it rose to popularity during Anne's reign in Great Britain during the first 10 years of 1700. The handgun was advanced for its day and led to a later advancement that, if it had been capitalized upon, would have changed warfare. Two features of the Queen Ann pistol set it apart from previous handguns and its contemporaries. First, its barrel was rifled, which gave the pistol greater accuracy and range. Second, the barrel didn't load from the muzzle like most firearms up until that point and for the 100 years afterwards, but from the breech. The barrel was threaded and unscrewed from the breechblock. A large chamber gave room to drop in a soft lead ball and a measured charge of powder. The rifling lands kept the slightly oversized ball from falling out of the barrel and the ball's soft lead consistency allowed it to swage in the rifling. The pistol was easy to load and clean, but was too expensive and had tolerances that were considered too tight to allow for military use.

Linear Tactics

Instead of breechloading rifles and rifled pistols, the standard weapons in the early 1700s were smoothbore muzzleloading muskets. The British Brown Bess went through several iterations, called patterns, but remained a .71-caliber smoothbore flintlock musket. The French version was a similar musket with steel bands holding the .69-caliber barrel to the wooden stock. The Charleville armory turned out these muskets, and gave them their name. Both muskets fitted a 12-inch triangular bayonet, which was a foundational part of warfare of the period.

Linear tactics, which were standard through the American Civil War, dictated that opposing armies line up on facing each other, march toward each other, and as the lines neared each other, begin firing volleys. After a few volleys, armies fixed bayonets and tried to sweep each other off the field. Nearly every battle ended with bayonets. The notorious inaccuracy of these rifles necessitated this type of linear warfare that seems insane when compared with modern tactics. The Brown Bess and Charleville muskets were accurate to only about 75 yards and they didn't have sights. Past that distance, a soldier was lucky to hit close to where he was aiming. The idea of firing volleys was to send a wall of lead downrange in the hopes that a shot aimed at one enemy soldier may miss him and still hit another enemy soldier. Standard cartridge boxes held only 20 or 30 shots because after a few shots, the black powder residue caked thick in the barrel's bores and made them difficult to load and on went the bayonets to finish the battle.

Rifle Versus Musket

For proper European gentlemen, aiming at one's enemy and shooting him was considered murder, even on the battlefield. Because of this attitude, weapons' accuracy wasn't a concern of military leaders. Hunting animals was different than killing humans, and the jaeger rifle was popular with German hunters. These guns were short, large-caliber rifles ornately decorated with engravings and inlays, and they were accurate enough to hit a pie plate at 100 yards with every shot. Loading was a somewhat slow process. First, the shooter measured the main powder charge and dumped it down the barrel. Then he spit on a cloth patch, which he placed over the muzzle and he set the soft lead ball over it. The shooter then short-started the ball with a special tool to leave the patched ball just beneath the muzzle and he cut off the excess cloth. This left the patch to act as a gasket to seal the gases from the burning powder when the gun was fired. The patch also helped the rifling grip the ball and impart spin on it. The shooter rammed the ball down and seated it on top of the powder charge and finally, he primed the flintlock pan with finely ground powder.

On the other hand, the musket was relatively quick to load. Whereas a rifle used a tight-fitting patch and ball that had to be rammed down, a military musket used a just an undersized ball that could sometimes be dropped down the barrel on top of the main charge. A well-trained soldier using a typical paper cartridge could fire three, sometimes four aimed shots in a minute with a musket. A rifleman could fire only twice in the same time. The musket had another advantage over the rifle — the rifle could not fit a bayonet and in hand-to-hand combat, when the musket could be a long spear, the rifle was just a big club. To compensate for this glaring shortfall of the rifle, American Benjamin Flowers designed and built a few hundred rifleman's folding pikes during the American Revolution for American riflemen. But since George Washington and most military leaders of the time preferred muskets to rifles, the idea didn't gain traction and there are no surviving samples of Flowers' invention. While legends talk about how Americans hid behind rocks and trees and shot the red-clad British regulars, that's not true. Americans used linear tactics the same as the British and when there were riflemen in a battle, they would be lined up next to musket-carrying soldiers.

Ferguson's Rifle

It wasn't until British Major Patrick Ferguson invented a breechloading rifle that fitted a bayonet that a rifle could compete with the musket on the battlefield of the 18th and 19th centuries. Ferguson's rifle resembled the British Brown Bess, and it fired the same ammunition, but because it had a different, multifunctional trigger guard, it had much greater accuracy, and boasted twice the rate of fire. Ferguson designed the rifle breech so it was threaded and rotated downward as the shooter rotated the trigger guard. Once the chamber was open, the soldier dropped in the ball, poured in the powder, rotated the bolt closed, primed the lock, and was ready to fire. The gun didn't need to be cast about, could be loaded while a soldier was laying down, and it didn't need a ramrod for loading, which shortened the reloading time so that most soldiers could get off six aimed accurate shots in a minute.

Ferguson performed firing tests of his rifle in 1776 at the England Arsenal and he even demonstrated the gun to King George III. The test included shots at 200 yards while stationary and four shots while advancing at the target. Then Ferguson wet the barrel's bore to simulate damp weather and then fired several shots to prove that the rifle would remain in working order. Unfortunately for Ferguson, his rifle didn't make financial sense to mass produce as it cost three times as much as the standard-issue Brown Bess. The rifle's screw breech mechanism, with its 12 to 14 grooves were difficult to machine, they gummed up quickly with burnt black powder residue, and the gun was generally difficult to clean. As a result, only between 100 and 200 copies of the rifles were built.

The Ferguson In Action

Ferguson's rifle saw action at one battle at Brandywine Creek near Philadelphia where Ferguson commanded 100 men carrying the rifle. Reports from the battle tell of the soldiers' effectiveness with the weapon, but they were only 100 men in a battle force of 30,000 British soldiers. Their small number undoubtedly diluted their possible influence. Ferguson himself could have changed the tide of the war, possibly even ending the war, during the battle. At one point, he saw an American general riding atop a white horse. Ferguson aimed his rifle at the officer, but didn't fire because he considered it ungentlemanly for an officer to shoot and kill an enemy officer. The general later turned out to be George Washington.

Ferguson was wounded at Brandywine and during his recovery, British General William Howe ordered his unit to be disbanded and his rifles stored away in a cellar in New York. Ferguson's soldiers were then reissued Brown Bess muskets. Historians blame this quick putting away of Ferguson's rifle, even after its strong performance at Brandywine, on Howe's admission that he was sympathetic to the American colonists' plight. Ferguson himself was shot dead off his horse three years later at the Battle of King's Mountain in 1780, a battle where British forces and American loyalists were surprised and suffered tremendous casualties in the hour-long battle.

Original Fergusons are extremely rare today, as the National Museum in Washington, D.C. owns two copies, one copy is housed in the Rudolph J. Nunnemacher Arms Collection in Milwaukee, and another is displayed at the West Point U.S. Military Academy museum. The U.S. National Park Service owns the last two and displays them at the southern American Revolution battle sites of Kings Mountain and at Cowpens, both in South Carolina.

In the end, Ferguson designed a solid weapon that suffered because it was ahead of its time. Standard-issue muskets wouldn't be rifled until the 1850s and breechloading rifles wouldn't be widespread for another 40 years. Military historians also argue that commanders in the 1700s didn't understand how to best utilize fast-loading weapons. These rifles might have turned the tide of the American Revolution if they had been produced in large enough quantities and had been used by the fast-moving cavalry.

Printed in Great Britain
by Amazon